Love is Strong as Death

My walk through the valley of its shadow

Rick and Nancy Fleeter

Outskirts Press, Inc.
Denver, Colorado

Since my freshman year at Brown University in 1972 through my teaching there today, I have felt a connection with the campus' Carrie Tower. Its emotional strength inspired me to believe its inscription, quoting the Bible's Song of Songs 8:6. As a student, I read it as instruction on the role of love in living. Confronting it now, not as theory but in the context of my life with Nancy, it has lost its authority. Now it questions me about the mystery of loss.

LOVE IS STRONG AS DEATH

Foreword

Nancy was first diagnosed in 1992. Over the next fifteen years we became veteran cancer patients. She was treated in Washington, DC, at hospitals in Fairfax, Virginia, and mostly at Sloan Kettering in New York. During the first ten years, cancer was more a routine task to attend to than a true illness. Then for four years it was more serious, with one or two surgeries per year. The last year or so was the most intense.

If I learned just one thing from the progress of the disease, it was from my brother, who said there is no such thing as having a little cancer—meaning one never knows—and that is also true for "healthy" people. It pays to be on guard and to take appropriate action. I have for many years had a very common precancerous condition of my facial skin, and I'm quite aggressive about treating it, even though most people might ignore it. At worst, my dermatologist will enjoy an extra ski trip on my account.

Nancy's outcome—well, I would describe it as tragic, though in the world of cancer she would be cataloged as successful, since that's the description applied to patients who survive more than five years after most diagnoses. We had fifteen years, most of that time healthy. During those many—and too few—years, the disease became a reason to pay more attention to each other and to the life we did have. I look back and regret how slowly I caught on, but when is it otherwise? We are always much wiser in hindsight, and no matter how smart I became how fast, it wouldn't have changed the course of things.

Many people have not even close to what we had between us, and given where we spent her time in treatment, we saw more than a person really wants to see. This was a help to Nancy—she realized early on that despite her situation, she was better off, had more time and a richer life, than so many others. As often is true in these situations, the victim achieves a higher state of accommodation than the caregiver. I take some comfort in that, since I cannot say I reached that level of acceptance—then nor now.

Writing this foreword months after Nancy's death, I have taken advantage of the new life I somehow parachuted into, one without responsibility for another life, to live, teach, write, and ride my bicycle around Rome, Italy, and coastal Rhode Island. I have moved out of the house where we lived for over twenty years in Virginia, and carry very few remembrances— photographs, a tiny porcelain urn of cremated remains, and her favorite menorah built out of a likeness of a racing bicycle—in suitcases with me as I roam earth's surface. It is a relief, though one I feel still some lingering guilt for enjoying, to concern myself with the mundane challenges of work and teaching and the imperfect subjunctive tense of various Italian verbs.

I am probably still not taking my share of responsibility for my extended family and other so-called obligations of adult life, but I have committed myself to not doing anything, nor being anywhere, that turns me back toward a state of mind I can't cope with. If I don't take care of my survival, physical and spiritual, I am no good to anyone else either. Escapism is preferable to the alternatives, and I highly recommend it as a lifestyle choice.

I don't think humans are built to address these big issues for too long nor for much time in a day. Nancy's death is never completely behind me, and in fact, it motivates many of the basics of my life's architecture. I realize that, and in a way I'm glad to have those structural limits. We all need some boundaries within which to place our focus. But work and the every day, *la vita quotidiana*, what used to bore me and wear me down, what I used to call the grind, are now a welcome relief. I wake up early to take advantage of every minute of every day. None of my heartbeats are wasted. None.

Some of these heartbeats I invest in thinking about our past, a thought process I started recording many years ago, before it became that past, and which is sampled in these pages in the hope that they may provide some boundaries, some signposts, for others who are following their own roads within this landscape.

Acknowledgements

Every book is a sum of experiences the author has with people, with God, with nature. How can I thank one part of that continuum above any other? Nancy and I were unusual. We were fortunate to have a medical team, family, clergy, and circle of friends who did nothing but support us during the most difficult of life's passages—dying way too young. I was lucky to have my other interests—in friends and family, in study, writing and music, in cycling and swimming, in language and travel, in aerospace design and teaching, to provide a basis for a life filled with distractions.

Along with every one of my family and circle of friends, most of whom appear in these essays, I would also have to thank the carbon Colnago bicycle parked in my apartment in Rome, my Speedo suit and goggles, my Neosport wet suit, always at the ready to attack the open Atlantic, and the 100+ students I have tried to be adequate to at Brown, at the Italian Space Agency, and at La Sapienza in Rome, for taking me out of myself—early each day and often. Without them, I don't like to think of where I'd be. AeroAstro, the company I founded in 1988, generously provided me sabbatical support that was the germ of this book. The company was the first element of the outside world to which I returned, just a week after Nancy's death.

It is this complex web I thank, in addition to these friends and family, all of whom are a part of this book:

My brother and sister-in-law, Tom and Joanne, my parents Hannah and Jerry, and my sister Carol.

Nancy's mother Anita, her sister Karen, and her twin Jeanne adopted our mission as their own. Nancy and I did not have that luxury of choice. The value of their dedication to physically being with us is beyond my ability to adequately acknowledge.

Nancy's hospice nurse, Colleen, was one of her angels, and Rabbi Steve was another. Both sat patiently with her, ready to whisper an inch from her ear when she would be capable of listening, communicating to her that most important message—you are not alone.

Nancy's faith in my nursing was not always 100%—she knew me too well. But she trusted our neighbor Susan, a nurse and a friend, always available to help, to provide the right advice and to supervise my technique.

Nancy's friends Ko and Diana each made 10-hour round trips on Amtrak and in taxis to see her for the few minutes her strength allowed.

Alan was the other man in Nancy's life, never failing to appear with just the right gift, words, or kiss on her cheek, and to rescue me so often from myself.

Nancy's ballet partner, Sheila, became my partner in establishing her legacy in dance, and thus became the embodiment of Nancy's future on earth.

David Ascalon of Ascalon Studios created the stained glass windows whose images decorate this book with the artist's generous permission which we gratefully acknowledge. Sunlight shines through the windows themselves at Temple Beth Emet, Herndon, Virginia.

Nancy, like so many cancer victims we met over the years spanned within this book, grew in strength as her physicality dissolved. Only seeing that miracle at close range can a person come to understand that we are more than our bodies, more than our physicality, and that the human spirit is more real, more important, and stronger than the illusions of the material. Reality, as we define it in daily life, is the ghost. The spirit is the only thing that is real. To come to know this beacon Nancy left for all of us who accompanied her, at least as far as we could, contrasted against the darkness of loss, is the gift I am most thankful for.

Hard Rain

Bicyclists know that cycling's an outdoor sport and you have to dress accordingly or wash out. Life is also an outdoor sport. Tough things happen, and sometimes nature is what we can only perceive as cruel. No matter how tough a situation you have been given, there are others carrying heavier burdens. Nancy knew this all too well, and had a defense mechanism— low expectations. Reality usually bettered any hopes she had for it. Even at the end, she believed she had at least had the chance to get over the difficult years and her fears.

Nancy had done the things she wanted to and lived. She never expected to have even that opportunity, and a longer life would have been a surprise to her.

My coping mechanism is to believe that things can and should be good, and if they're bad now, it's only a matter of waiting. Bad times are a test of endurance, as in cycling.

While both philosophies work, I've come over somewhat to Nancy's prism. A hard rain is going to fall on all of us. We just don't know when, how often, or how hard. Your savings can be lost in a fraud or a lawsuit, and it's back to work as a greeter at Walmart at age 75. Houses burn down or get washed away by hurricanes. Car accidents, medical calamities—they are all possibilities.

So what's the strategy? Fly carefully.

Jim

Maybe growing up, as I did, on a steady diet of cartoons from my parents' *New Yorker* subscriptions, explains for me Nancy's attraction to a certain population of men, depicted in those black and white figures and their one line captions as older, financially established members of exclusive, politically incorrect clubs, to which they are delivered by their drivers from the back seats of large, ecologically incorrect dark colored sedans, to eat blood red in the center steaks preceded only by iceberg lettuce-wedge salads, drink Scotch or Bourbon, and smoke cigars. Men who vote straight Republican and vacation without their wives, with guides in Land Rovers, in Africa and South America, hunting big game. Not that Nancy supported many of these vices, herself an animal lover, Democrat to the core, insistent on vacationing with me, generally bothered by even cigarette smoke, and when she drove at all, it was in a VW Beetle. Nancy wouldn't spend an hour in the bush, even to photograph an animal. Though she did appreciate an occasional steak at Morton's preceded by a peaty single malt and being a guest in that smoky men's club exclusivity she admired.

But these men, and they were all men, from the cynical board members of *New Yorker* cartoons plotting their next corporate takeover to the cigared denizens of summer hunting mansions with animal busts jutting from raw-hewn walls, combined intelligence, power, and the freedom only an excess of money can provide, with the self confidence to be and act just as wrongly or rightly as they pleased. Working in the world of finance for some of the United States' major fine arts institutions provided

Nancy the perk of spending time in the company of these people who in a previous era would have been labeled tycoons. They were a surrogate for the self-confidence, freedom, and security she simultaneously dared not even aspire to, and resented, because of their excesses and their occasional indulgence in simple idleness.

Few of the real individuals she met of this ilk, the men who put money into her arts institutions and whose wives put time into their executive committees, whose names were at the top of the wall of golden circle donors in the biggest type sizes, whose companies advertised in the playbill, and whose pictures appeared in the Society section of the Sunday *Times*, lived up to the *New Yorker's* Fantasies. They were human. Up close she saw they too had weaknesses, even if only that of just trying too hard to be what they were. Most simply lacked that lack of desire she so desired.

But if there were one epitome, to her it was Jim. I know only a little about him. He was a self-made millionaire who then married into a much bigger fortune, which he neither needed nor cared about, except to complain about its burdens, which accrued more to his wife than to him directly. Jim was 20 years older than Nancy, tall and lanky, or so she said, since I never met him. He didn't really run his banking firm any more, delegating mostly to others, but he stayed somehow involved, sat on boards, cared for an infirm adult daughter, belonged to clubs, and invited Nancy to join him sometimes, I suppose on evenings when women were permitted as guests of the members. He hunted all over the world and had never met a Republican he didn't like. He and Nancy shared a love and a knack for finance. Nancy sometimes would call Jim to help her break a financial logjam, or think through a strategy to pull some financially devastated nonprofit from the brink. Or just to argue about where the markets were going and which political candidate was more certain to destroy the economy once and for all.

I think women instinctively understand that men, some men anyway, will always have an eye for an attractive female. They wouldn't say so, but they know it's the sign of a healthy male psyche. And I considered Nancy's attraction to self-made, uninhibited, powerful older men of the upper class to be similarly a sign of a healthy female psyche. ì

Whatever the underlying psychology, biology, anthropology, and Darwinian logic, I encouraged her to enjoy these chances to spend time with the upper crust of the other half, which isn't really a half, but an esoteric, infinitesimal fraction of a percent of the world's population. Being chief of the green eyeshade brigade in the guts of a huge performing arts center, spending twelve- and often fourteen-hour days in windowless offices tucked up against the IBM mini mainframe with its whirring hard drives, high speed printers, cooling fans, and elevated flooring to accommodate all the power cords and cables is otherwise sorely lacking in, to put it politely, *je ne sais quoi*.

A few of these men telephoned from their cars and offices to check on Nancy during her illness. Many sent flowers regularly, or their wives or secretaries did, and several came to visit. Jim was one of the telephoners, and he was Nancy's favorite. I knew she was seriously ill when I took his call and she asked me to say she'd have to call back another time. That happened, I think, twice, and after that, I don't remember him calling again.

While writing this book, I took over one of Nancy's old computers, a Macintosh laptop she had custom-painted in metallic purple with a contrasting white keyboard and track pad. This was her travel machine for use on airliners, and it mainly saw duty as a DVD player. As she got weaker, she used the laptop at home to watch DVDs from her hospital-style bed because it was lighter and easier for her to manage.

Other than a few iTunes movies, there were no files on it, except for two. The first was a journal article on her disease, vulvar cancer, written by one of her doctors from Memorial Sloan-Kettering. I read it. Clinical. Nancy had a disease that fewer than a tenth of one percent of cancer patients get, and an even smaller fraction of that small group "experience mortality" from it. She was, in yet another way, one in a million.

The other file was labeled Private Letter. I am guessing it was never printed nor sent.

Dear Jim,

I have no idea why I'm writing this other than I've been a bit emotional over the last two months. I so appreciate your calls. It helps me to know you're thinking about me. I'm scared. I'm scared I won't make it and I don't know what that means. I don't know what happens after we die and I'm not ready to leave this earth yet.

I try to keep positive but it's difficult when I feel so lousy. I'm enjoying the time off … I've been working since I was seventeen … I enjoy having the time to read the NY *Times* every day and *The Economist* cover to cover. The time passes; I'm not particularly bored, Just apprehensive because I don't know what's happening next. All my life I've tried to do the right thing in order to prevent bad things from happening, and this … this I don't have control over.

Promise me one thing … that if it comes to it you'll come say good-bye?

—Nancy

November 5, 2003
… As seen from room 1930 at Memorial Sloan Kettering Cancer Center

I don't want to bore people with medical details, but I did get a number of email and voice mail requests for an update on how Nancy is doing. I'm guessing not because my commentaries are such glittering prose. So, thanks for your interest.

The number of I/O ports affixed to Nancy is down to just two, about a third of where we were a couple days ago. There's talk of sending Nancy home to our apartment here in Manhattan Thursday or Friday, albeit with a visiting nurse and a few tubes attached. I wonder how we manage that in a NYC cab?

Nancy is definitely in surgery recovery mode, taking the short walks around the floor, learning how hard it is to stand up, and dealing with having people to do things for her for a while. It's frustrating, but transient. She's in a chair a couple hours a day, and then back to the bed. She talks on the phone just a little. I shield her. I'm employed as her personal secretary.

There are a couple issues left. The big one is the pathology report, which the Doc believes will show good margins. Secondly, we have to keep the various incisions, and parts that have to grow back, clean. No infections yet.

The penthouse of Memorial Sloan Kettering is an interesting place. Most of the patients look like Nancy, shuffling around the corridor in the standard-issue Frette bathrobe while clinging to their IV poles. However, one guy has his staff constantly surrounding him, bearing Blackberries and cell phones. He dresses in his own tailored black pajamas, Darth Vader-esque shoes, no IV, and plenty of hair. I think he has cancer of the toenail, but I'm not sure. He meets his staff and visitors for lunches in the lounge. The women are all x-rays (people who look like the x-rays of other people), and the men are in business suits. Way too healthy. Whatever he does have, you probably don't want it.

Nancy's room is filled with flowers—ballet people are into flowers. We probably need to go home before she decides she likes the room better than home, and before we run out of money. I thought I had a cold, but maybe it's just pollen allergy. If we can maintain her current rate of progress, we'll be very grateful.

Will report any news as it happens. Thanks to all for the emails—I've been verbally relaying them to Nancy.

—Rick

Longing To Return

November 7, 2003

The trouble with these updates is, if I don't continue them, I might leave your imagination to its own devices. So let's agree this is the last one for a while, hopefully a long while, and control of your inbox I'll cede to the sexual organ enlargement and home mortgage spammers.

It took ten hours yesterday, but Memorial Sloan-Kettering Cancer Center finally released us at 5:30 last night. Last time we were there was the January blizzard of '03. Given there were not only no cabs, but no buses and really no traffic plying the briefly all white and sparkling island of Manhattan then, we slipped some sweat clothes over Nancy and started walking for the subway, which was six blocks away, in hip-deep snow. In her condition, it was what some have called a long, hard slog, so at least I have appreciation for that popular turn of phrase.

We found a cab right outside the Metro Station and made the mistake of taking it. An hour later, we completed the forty blocks home. That, too, was a long, hard slog, come to think of it. Ever the pilot/meteorologist, I had called Nancy's doc the night before and suggested, given the ominous weather forecast for the biggest storm of the decade, maybe a 7:30 a.m. discharge wouldn't be a bad idea. Too few doctors, I find, are meteorologists. Maybe they should offer pilot training in med school, since everything else is worked into the curriculum anyway.

But I digress. There wasn't a blizzard last night. Instead, we were discharged into rush hour in the rain, into the rainy New York gestalt of thousands of cabs driving by, but none available. General traffic, buses, and limos idled in long lines while waiting for more opportunities to get nowhere fast. The so-called transportation department at the hospital maintained its perfect record of failing to deliver, and instead, recommended we wait until 8:00 p.m., which meant sitting two-and-a-half hours in the lobby with Nancy in a wheelchair with her grenade thingy draining, catheter, wound in need of fresh dressing, and general state of fatigue. Not to mention four bags and backpacks full of stuff to lug home.

My chivalry was awakened and I did what any Lord Raleigh of the twenty-first century would do in such a situation—got on the cell phone. I reached a couple American Ballet Theater board members, and within twenty minutes, not one, but *two* limos showed up. We took the cushier one and sat on York Avenue for a long time, again a long, hard slog, but at least we were dry. Somehow a shared experience outside the hospital is always better than any experience inside. We passed the time as any modern couple would—each on our own cell phone handling crises from our offices and sending text messages.

Speaking of long, hard slogs, twice a day, we, and I do mean we, change two dressings and flush a catheter bag and this little grenade thing attached to a tube that disappears into her leg someplace. We're also keeping a bunch of pills straight and trying not to stress those little staples too much, as they seem to be the only boundary between the outside world and a lot of anatomy we don't want to know about. We take little walks up and down our corridor, and otherwise, just enjoy being not attached to an IV pole and at home in apartment 32H with a good view of midtown. Nan is still sleeping more than usual, probably due to her remaining pain med, and it's tiring doing the ADL (activities of daily living) thing when you haven't been up and around for ten days.

The visiting nurse came by today to get us into that program. We reported no serious need other than to make sure we were not messing things up particularly badly. She was okay with that, looked around the apartment, and gave Nancy the benefit of her experience: whatever you do, don't be riding those bicycles. Nancy assured her two of them were mine and the other one was for the stuffed animals to stay in shape with. She noted that in her book. I shouldn't pick on her. She was a big help, very sweet, and spent more than she earned visiting us to park in the garage in our building. But I did enjoy her obvious wondering how the two of us and all those bikes and animals lived in this broom closet.

Cancer-wise, we've emerged from yet another episode, but I think Nancy feels intuitively that it's never cured. It just attenuates from acute to chronic. She'll heal for a couple months, then radiation treatment, then just vigilance. If that vigilant stage lasts long enough, I think we'll consider the episode behind us. That's where Lance Armstrong got before he won his first Tour de France. We're back to wondering about next summer's triathlon circuit in Zürich, which might be hard to beat.

As I watch Nancy asleep on the couch or immersed in telephone conversation with work, trying to make up for not being there with only partial, frustrating success, it strikes me that, like so many cancer patients, she did nothing to end up with all these "procedures" (docs are as loathe calling an operation an operation as politicians are to call a war a war), missing a couple parts of her body and in lousy shape for weeks at a time. Unlike me, she doesn't go out and mix it up with trucks and teenage drivers on the road, spinning out twenty-five miles per hour on a seventeen-pound bike. She just works hard at supporting ballet and the arts. Nancy is pretty much content to come home to her five hundred square feet and twelve-inch TV with an order-in of Mexican from Baby Bo's on Lex.

I think our society has a tendency to believe that somehow we all deserve our fate—a particularly Christian ethic, maybe epitomized best in the early days of AIDS when it was seen by some in the United States as God directly punishing homosexual men. To help put our own situation in another perspective, my Mom sent me a book on the life and impact of Abraham. Abraham's message is the contrary—stuff happens. Abraham was maybe the first existentialist. Sometimes we deserve what we get, but more often, we just get what we get, good and bad. Did Bill Gates deserve to be worth $60 billion, and did Vincent Van Gough deserve to nearly starve?

We aren't worth $60 billion, but we aren't starving, and Nancy is going to do fine, regardless of our cosmic balance sheet of what is owed, deserved, and delivered. Whatever it is, we have more than we can appreciate, and that's true of almost everyone on the planet. What we can appreciate is everybody's interest and well wishes. We have enough flowers here to create a float for the Rose Bowl Parade. Nancy assures me her company can't fire her while she gets one percent better per day, so we're enjoying an opportunity to do a little project together in medical technology. We'd rather be maybe redecorating our kitchen, but whatever.

—Rick

March 15, 2006
Nancy got into surgery at Sloan-Kettering close to 5:00 p.m., four hours after the scheduled time. We had awaited the surgery in her luxo room in the penthouse, so that wasn't too bad. Nancy is a good sport, having not had even water since yesterday. She's become a veteran patient here.

I just spoke with her surgeon, Liz, around 6:30 p.m. She said that on the negative side, things had grown significantly since the biopsy a month ago, but on the good side, not enough to require the plastic surgeon. So, the surgery was a little over an hour and no additional surgical work was needed for now.

Liz felt the rash Nancy's had was unlikely to be cancer-related. It more likely is from hormonal therapy she has since discontinued. Liz agreed with Tom's diagnosis and treatment and felt that chapter was probably over. The rash and other symptoms are completely gone as of yesterday and today.

Going forward, Liz also felt that the important thing is to keep close watch on Nancy and do a minisurgery ASAP if anything shows up. The doctor felt this is normal for what Nancy has been treated for, and could go on essentially forever without becoming anything more serious, so long as they keep watching it. We will probably move that watching to Reston, but we can think about that later.

I'll go meet Nancy in recovery around 8:00 p.m. and then probably take off for our hotel until tomorrow morning. With luck, we'll get out of the hospital tomorrow, but that's yet to be decided. The current plan is to drive to Reston on Saturday, but we can postpone to Sunday if necessary.

I'll report further details if there are any, but probably no more tonight.

—Rick

August 5, 2007

My "vacation" next week will be at the luxury spa known as Reston Hospital. I will begin chemotherapy treatment on Monday. I would not have said anything, but Rick felt I should, and unless I had suddenly developed the desire to be a Britney Spears look-alike, it will be fairly obvious that my hair (which, I might add, I spend hundreds of dollars on each year getting cut and colored!) will be gone. This won't be easy, which is why I will not be in contact next week ... I plan to watch movies and sit with Lulu. Any questions on business items please ask Kris or Rick. Thanks.

—Nancy

Courtesy David Ascalon of Ascalon Studios

Pillar of Fire

August 7, 2007
Nancy's not dead, but if you didn't know that, you might think so.

I got home from meetings with Radyne, the company that is buying our company, at about 6:00 p.m. I woke her up on the couch and she said, "How did you get home so early? " I had to point out it was 6:00 p.m. She hadn't moved since I left at 7:30 a.m. and hadn't eaten even the plain toast that I left. She had just been lying there for ten hours, only waking up to take medicine. She's taking five different drugs, including Vicodan, to prevent problems with her digestive system, which has been hit fairly hard by the chemo. Nancy has really cut back on the Vicodan. She's down from twelve a day to maybe four or five per day. No explanation for that.

Tom thinks if I can get Nancy to eat five hundred calories per day, that's pretty good. She can't handle even white toast or white rice. Chicken soup, no noodles, and cranberry juice are about all. She'll start to improve on Saturday, so it really doesn't matter much and I think we're making it to the five-hundred number.

Other than no energy or appetite, she's okay. As usual, when the doc said, "Well, you probably won't feel like going to work that first week," it was a bit of an understatement. We have a midweek checkup tomorrow, but apparently Nancy is doing pretty well, as these things go.

What a system—it's known as slash, burn, and poison. Accurate.

—Rick

August 18, 2007

Very quick update. I don't want to update you only when things are tough—so the message today is that eight days after the first round of chemotherapy was completed, Nancy is recovering into her old self. She's really happy to have some energy and appetite, though she's still quite weak, which anyone would be after twelve days being horizontal for any reason.

So now we are looking forward to nine days of relative normalcy before round two starts on the twenty-seventh. We'll see if/when she has enough gazorch to get in a car and be driven to work, but at least she feels well and can do a little computer and mail work. Her philosophy right now is along the lines of "one day at a time."

Nancy's mother is flying in on the twenth-fifth to help her through the next treatment.

Thanks for your emails and thoughts. I'll probably not bug you until sometime into round II. We don't expect the second course to be as bad because Nancy has adapted to the treatment itself, and because we have figured out the right drugs and doses to control symptoms. The first time is a lot of trial and error—and as that cliché implies, the number of errors is almost equal to the number of trials.

—Rick

September 9, 2007
It is a little strange to report on treatment of a disease as news, especially serially, but here goes. Take three.

After a couple weeks to recuperate, Nancy started round II (like that Super Bowl allegory) two weeks ago. While it's hard to compare, it's safe to say that treatment week was no easier than round I. This time, we tried her spending a few nights in the hospital to get continuous hydration. The result was the same sick patient as last time, except hydrated. Maybe bravado on my part, but while I can't match the hydration power of a 0.9% saline IV drip, holistic care it wasn't. By leaving her connected to the IV, she really couldn't be bothered with ambulation, which is not good. The food was quite laughable, given what I knew about Nancy's recent transformation into a finicky eater. The patient, who has a hard time swallowing even a pill, and has to be coaxed to ingest a spoonful of dilute yogurt, was served a Western omelet for breakfast, beef stew for lunch, etc.

The good news of that week was Anita, Nancy's mom, flew in from LA and sat with her both at home and at the hospital, which allowed me to make a quick business trip to Phoenix and LA. The hospital meal service at least saved Anita from needing to commute down to the hospital cafeteria. Food wasn't wasted—it just didn't reach its intended destination. However, it really doesn't matter. At that stage for Nancy, there's really not much hope of her eating anyway. It doesn't pay to obsess about appetite. It returns when it's ready.

Nancy came home a week ago Friday, when Anita and I were both around to arrange her discharge and to take care of her at home. This past week she's become increasingly more comfortable, eating and drinking, at first minimal amounts but now close to normal. Externally, Nancy looks good. Her hair and skin look fine, and her thinness is not quite at the Vogue model level, but she's definitely on the thin side compared with her normal weight.

Occasionally Nancy has enough energy to talk on the phone, but that's rare, and my job of shielding her from the phone and visitors is secure for the time being. She doesn't read email, but she does read the cards that everybody sends. I still recommend that as the best way to give her a pick-me-up. Nancy is a dedicated reader, and as soon as she has a speck of energy, she picks up her cards and books.

This week we're hoping she might have the energy to even get to the office once or twice. Now that she's been through two rounds of treatment, she has some tests scheduled to see if the tumors are shrinking. The expressed "wisdom" of her MD is that there are three possibilities—shrinking, status quo, and growing. With the first two possibilities indicative of success, she has a two in three chance of a good test. They tell you medicine is as much art as it is science, and I believe this small example indicates that duality. I'm about to go to the pool for my daily one km swim, where I may either drown or not drown, so yeah, I guess I have a fifty/fifty chance of a good outcome.

Actually, Nancy's doc is a great person, and it's a pleasure to see him. His point is, nobody really knows how effective any treatment will be, and Nancy is fine with that. We're getting by day-to-day, minimizing the bad parts and enjoying what can be taken from the experience, which is not a huge set, but neither is it an empty one. If we find out the treatment isn't working, there are alternative drugs so she would switch. But the current regimen appears to have reduced her pain and we think it is working, in which case round III begins on Monday the seventeenth. That will be the beginning of another tough seven to ten days again. Most patients get three to six rounds, so again, there's no real plan. We'll just get through round III and then make new decisions.

Like starting school, or a vacation, or a new job, eventually almost anything reduces to a routine, and that's where we are now. The big questions can't be addressed every day, and the little ones have all been answered, so we just do it and there's no drama. Thanks to Anita, our housekeeper, whom we share with my brother's family, I'm able to get to work and go on the occasional bike ride because Nancy always has someone here or immediately on hand.

As usual, I hope this note is interesting and helpful, and I welcome any feedback or questions. Next update in a couple weeks, or sooner if any newsworthy events occur.

—Rick

September 23, 2007

To paraphrase, I'd like to stop meeting like this. Illness does have a way of bringing people together, but next time I think we'd prefer to just do lunch.

Last update was a little over two weeks ago. Since then, Nancy had a few further complications from her treatment. She had a blood clot last weekend, which resulted in her coming back to Reston Hospital on Saturday night via the ER. We were lucky we took it seriously; she got treated immediately, and though she had to spend the next six days in the hospital, there will be no permanent damage.

She's back at home now, has some lingering discomfort from that whole episode, but glad to be home, mostly comfortable, and we're back to managing things as before. Her appetite has improved, and she looks pretty much as she did before the chemo treatments. Given all the ups and downs, we agreed she would go on short-term disability from work—we are lucky to have excellent insurance in this regard. We'll focus on getting Nancy better and getting her treated.

Unfortunately, the side effects from her chemo treatments represented a case of pain but no gain. Like surgery and radiation, the chemo provided some temporary suppression, but with no apparent lasting effect. And like surgery and radiation, chemo is not something you can keep doing forever—it *has* to have a lasting effect.

So this week we embark on another phase. Layperson that I am, I don't know exactly what you'd call it: medication-based treatment? There are several drugs that suppress the cancer, so long as the patient stays on them. But since they are pretty easily tolerated, patients simply stick with their drug over a very long term. The decision now is mainly which drug and then to learn all the details of the treatment. We have an appointment at Georgetown to look into a couple of possibilities this week. Nancy's main oncologist has a few other suggestions, and we will also pay a visit to Johns Hopkins in Baltimore. We're also getting suggestions by remote control from New York and Boston. But like chemo, choosing a medication is far from a science. Trial and error is not so bad if you're Thomas Edison looking for the right filament for a light bulb, but it's hard on live patients. The good news is we have a long list of options to try.

Meanwhile, at least Nancy is home, recovering from chemo, improving daily, and mostly comfortable. Lulu the cat is much happier now that she's back. As am I.

Nancy has had only two visitors and that was about all she could handle. So while I'm sorry to always ask the same, she's enjoying receiving cards and notes more than anything else.

After we do the medical visits of the week, I'm heading off to Phoenix for two days of meetings. Nancy's sister, Karen, is arriving Tuesday and will stay with her while I'm gone.

One thing I remember from my mini-career as a pilot—once the weather turns lousy, it doesn't pay to check the ceiling and visibility every hour. Weather has its pace, and so does medical treatment. Treatment, especially trial and error, and eventually healing, take time. Nancy is much more patient than I am—I'd be frustrated, to say the least, in her situation. She's calm and realizes the timing of things, and she focuses on day-by-day. She gets an A as a patient. And we've been really happy with the nursing and physician care and attention she's getting. Every step has been well thought out, and any problems have been worked out promptly. In addition, everyone's supportive. No complaints, other than we need her to get better.

We're working on that part. As my thesis advisor always added to the ends of my sentences pledging to get "our" work done: Assiduously!

—Rick

September 25, 2007

The strategy now is that they are going to do five intense radiation doses to try to kill off the one tumor that is causing all the trouble in the upper leg by the hip joint. Nancy's cancers are all benign, except if they grow somewhere inconvenient. So if they can zap this one it would solve all the current problems—the leg swelling, groin pain, and her immobility. Since it's blocking the main vein returning blood from the leg, it's probably why her clot is so slow to clear, and why she is so sore to stand.

From thirty-five thousand feet, this is really back to the basics we've been doing for ten years—take out bothersome growths as they happen and life then goes on until the next crisis, which can be years away. The downside is getting her to the hospital five days in a row (Wednesday, Thursday, and Friday, then Monday and Tuesday.) Karen will take her in the mornings. Nancy has decided, which I support, as does Janet, the doc, while doing the radiation, that she be re-admitted into the hospital at least until Friday afternoon. This way she doesn't have to be transported back and forth to the hospital. The pain is so intense to move her that even all the drugs won't hide the pain, and why put her through that six times this week?

If she's a little better by Friday, she can come home for the weekend. If not, she'll stay there.

With any luck, five days of two hours irradiation per day will diminish the tumor and give her and her vein some relief.

I have set up home health care, but we'll postpone that until Nancy's back home again. The home health available to her is excellent, so I'm glad to have gotten that help ready when we need it. Also, Karen is here and knows most of the basics, and our neighbor, Susan, will be by in the mornings for Nancy's next Lovinox. I did tonight's already and renewed her seventy-two hour patch. While she's in the hospital, Susan and Anita will have a few days' respite.

We are going through pre-authorization with Blue Cross for the Tarceva, which will then start the day after the radiation ends. The docs agreed not to do radiation and medication simultaneously, because together put too much load on an already weakened person. Practically speaking, it will be Monday before they are ready to start Tarceva, so, it's a two-day delay at most. Possibly Nancy's insurance will cover the Tarceva, and if not, we'll pay for it for a while and see if it works. If it does work, we'll find a way to get it more or less economically. We'll be lucky to have that problem. BTW to Tom: Janet mentioned to me that she has also heard some good things about the Tarceva and is hopeful this is a good application for it. She is probably reading the same reports you and I are.

I hope this all works. It's heart-breaking to see Nancy in this condition. She's really suffering, and those few moments when she's comfortable are just a tease between crises. That's no way to live, and although she is going to be in quite a bit of pain just getting to the hospital, hopefully that's short-term for longer-term improvement.

—Rick

October 7, 2007
Since it's only been two weeks since the last update, I wouldn't be bugging you again so soon, except I'm on a little campaign for Nancy's birthday, which is coming up on the eighteenth of this month.

In her current condition, the usual spectrum of birthday presents and events—cake, clothes, jewels, party, dinner out, etc.—none of them makes sense. Instead, working with some of Nancy's friends, we have established a fund in her name at Maryland Youth Ballet (MYB; more about the company at http://www.marylandyouthballet.org/).

MYB is primarily a school for young dancers, and it also supports a large population of adults. It is the premier dance school in the Northern Virginia/Maryland DC region, and has graduated several dancers to American Ballet Theater, New York City Ballet, and other internationally recognized companies. Nancy has been a board member of MYB and their CFO pro bono.

Despite all that it has done, like almost all arts organizations, MYB operates on the narrowest margins. Coming into this year's season, the company was forced by its fiscal constraints to once again recycle costumes which, to be polite, are several years beyond their sell-by date. They don't look professional, and they are difficult to even don, yet alone dance in.

We created the Nancy Fleeter Costume Fund to make new costumes available for this season and hopefully beyond. Thanks to friends of Nancy at MYB who helped establish the fund, plus my own gift, I'm pleased to report that we have about reached the minimum we'll need to meet the most urgent needs. There are two reasons I'd like you to consider donating. One is that the costuming needs of the company easily exceed the basic level of funding already committed. Secondly, costumes are needed for additional performances and to upgrade costumes beyond those of just the principle dancers.

From your point of view, if you're thinking of doing something for Nancy's birthday, which is October 18, I'd like to make this option available to you. However, it is important to me that nobody feels pressured to donate. This is strictly if you would like to do something for Nancy on her birthday and would like to use her costume fund at MYB as that way of expressing yourself. Donations will be appreciated, and I am staying involved in how MYB uses the money to ensure that 100% of the donations are applied to upgrading costumes.

MYB is a 501(c)3 charitable organization, and as you won't receive an MYB tote bag or coffee mug, 100% of any donation is tax deductible. You will receive a letter receipt from MYB for your donation. On her birthday, Nancy will be presented with a framed sample of the new costumes, hand-sewn in miniature, roughly the scale of a Barbie® outfit—and a card signed by the staff at MYB. Until then, she will know nothing about the fund.

If you decide you'd like to support the Nancy Fleeter Costume Fund at Maryland Youth Ballet, all you need to do is send a check for any amount to: Sheila Riley, 4514 Connecticut Avenue, Suite 409, Washington DC 20008.

The check should be written to Maryland Youth Ballet, and in the comments section write Nancy Fleeter Costume Fund.

Thanks for any and all support. I know it will help make MYB a stronger institution, which has been a campaign of Nancy's and many of her friends there. The establishment of the fund will give Nancy even more than it gives to MYB.

—Rick

November 3, 2007

As the weather cools, days shorten, leaves fall, and football eclipses baseball, I can't help think the Super Bowl is not far off. Hence I'm abandoning the Roman numerals when I talk about rounds of treatment. Super Bowl this year is at XLII. I hope I don't end up writing that many updates.

Part of the reason for the long interval is that life has been blissfully routine since the end of September. Nancy has been at home, with no major crises, while slowly recovering from chemo, the blood clot, and her radiation, as well as the cancer itself.

She had a week of radiation treatment at Reston Hospital, which appears to have, at least for now, brought her a lot of relief and eliminated the immediate sense of crisis. My lay interpretation is that radiation works, the problem being it can't always be used everywhere you need it, so it's just one of several necessary treatments. In Nancy's case, having eliminated chemo, the rest of her treatment includes Tarceva, which is somewhat effective on other types of cancers. It is being used only experimentally for Nancy's specific brand of the disease.

It's a good thing from the point of view of our insurance company, which doesn't have to pay for the pills. Since though Tarceva is pretty widely used for this disease, it is still an "off label" application. As my brother points out, instead of sending a kid to Harvard, we are sending money to Genentec (indirectly via a pharmacy). You have to burn through a compact car's dollar value in the drug before anybody knows if it is actually working, but so far, so good. If it really does work, Nancy would just stay on it forever and transition back to normal life. To me it's reminiscent of the early AIDS drugs—they worked, but only some people could afford them. But this is much simpler than those drugs—just one little pill, once a day. I think the least Genentec could do is provide a credit for a week at their own beach club in Hawaii or St. John for every year you consume their product. Maybe I'll suggest this on their web site.

Over the last week, Nancy has been able to spend a few minutes on the phone and email, but not much since her energy is almost undetectable and easily spent. She is still in bed all day except for a few minutes to shower or walk a few steps. She's doing physical therapy to try to get back in shape.

I know she's gotten many cards, but I don't open them—just deliver. So if you've been sending them, thanks! I know Nancy is opening and reading every one, but I'm pretty sure she's not responding. I've been advising her to enjoy getting mail and not worry about answering it.

The big event over the last month was Nancy's birthday and the presentation of her gift by Sheila Riley and Ned Kraft. I know most of the people on this email list contributed to the costume fund at Maryland Youth Ballet, and I can report that we raised a substantial war chest for building new costumes. Nancy was totally surprised and really pleased. Sheila gave Nancy a tiny costume—big enough for maybe a large mouse—on a small pink hanger to illustrate what the gift was about. Sheila and Ned also brought champagne to the bedside, though Nancy's portion was only used to clink glasses. Her metabolism is barely handling plain cottage cheese for now. It was, I think, the most fun Nancy has had in a few months. Thanks to everyone for helping make this possible—it meant a lot to Nancy and to MYB.

Our immediate plans are, as they have been forever, take it one day at a time and slowly recover. We are hoping to be able to drive to Rhode Island for Christmas, but we'll need to see how things go in the next four to six weeks to know if that's a possibility. Nancy's in remarkably good spirits considering how long she's been stuck in that bed. I respect her patience—she keeps busy mostly with reading, the computer, net surfing, and DVD watching.

More news as I have any to report. Meantime, keep those cards and prayers coming.

—Rick

December 11, 2007

My biological interval timer is nudging me—time for another update! The last one was November 3, a little over five weeks ago. This one will be shorter, which is a good thing.

Nancy's condition is a sort of weighted average of test results and how she feels. The test results look good, or at least not bad, and she's feeling progressively better. In this race, one can ultimately never completely win. Being ahead is about as good as it gets.

Test-wise, there does not appear to be any new growth, and possibly there is some death of tumor cells. We don't know if that's for sure, and if it is, we don't know why it's happening. Radiation or the new drug are our best guesses. Nancy's going back for more imaging in January, a longer interval since her treatments, and we hope for a more conclusive read. My own theory is that for all the time we've dealt with the disease, twelve-plus years, Nancy has been her own best barometer. When it kicks up, she starts feeling lousy long before the doctors and machines can find anything. When she feels good, she is good.

Having spent the time since July mostly horizontal in a hospital bed, Nancy is pretty weak. Her physical therapist comes twice a week, and I have started taking her for water walking and stretching in the pool on two other days. I can't say she exactly looks forward to immersion in cold chlorinated water—who does? But it's definitely helping to rev her engines up a little. She takes a couple trips up the stairs every day, fetches a lot of her own food, and spends a lot of time not in bed—on a couch or big chair. She can ride comfortably stretched out in the car. This is not the picture of perfect health, but it's a big step up from where we were just a few weeks ago.

Nancy looks like her old self and sounds like herself. She can finally taste food again and is eating a slightly wider variety of foods, which leads us both to conclude that for now, the game is recovery. If the drugs and/or radiation can keep her cancer at bay, I think things will just continue trending toward normalcy. She's even talking about driving her car again some day in the maybe distant but at least foreseeable future.

Pilots are very careful not to tempt Murphy and his laws. They say, "If all goes well, we'll be on the ground by 8:00 p.m." My caveat is, "For now ... ." Nobody really understands this disease, and we sure don't. And nobody has a crystal ball—except maybe the Wicked Witch of the West—who had an identity and a fate few aspire to. Nancy and I are focused on doing what we can every day, enjoying what we can each day, and hoping for continued good results. Good things can and sometimes do happen. We're open to that possibility. In the meantime, life is maybe a little bland, but enjoyable and comfortable. Bland Is sometimes a good thing.

Our house in Rhode Island is slowly emerging from its reconstruction as a sunny and rejuvenated place, and when it's ready for noncontractor human occupants, we're ready to spend some time there—probably early in '08. If Nancy can ride four hundred miles in the Jetta and get up the stairs to our house, which is on stilts, would be one sign of her improvement, and one of the many things we're looking forward to resuming and doing together.

Both of us wish the best of this season and Happy New Year to all. And when my internal alarm goes off again—probably in January—I'll send what news we've got. Thanks for your continuing thoughts and cards—still the best treat Nancy gets every day.

—Rick

December 14, 2007
I apologize for not showing up for the AeroAstro '07 Christmas party today.

Our surprise was going to be that Nancy was joining me. We were in the Jetta, dressed for Christmas (sort of), toting our Secret

Santa gift, plus a disc of Christmas music and the electronics and speakers to play them with, plus some additional edibles. As we were waiting for the left turn light into our office park, a call from one of Nancy's many MDs resulted in a U-turn (at least I was in the appropriate lane). Next stop was the emergency entrance at Reston Hospital.

I don't know who of us was more disappointed (I think that's the most polite way to put it) at sitting yet again in the ER awaiting admission, going through the red tape, getting the bracelet, taking vital signs for the 29,000th time, and getting wheeled into a bay to await blood tests and yet another doctor's visit.

Very little of our time is actually spent dealing with cancer. It's spent dealing with side effects of treatments. This time it was some suspicious bleeding, which is a side effect of Tarceva. It inhibits skin growth, and if you have a weakness, like where you've had surgery and radiation, you can get problems. No big deal, as it turned out, but they wanted to be sure what was going on. Reasonable, but still not your most enjoyable Friday afternoon.

Scarcely six hours later, we got permission to go home. That's a mere blink of the eye, a medical femtosecond, particularly by ER standards, and highly preferable to a weekend in a hospital room somewhere. Somehow we didn't feel particularly elated by our good fortune. But at least both of us are safe and sound again, with just a few new things to take care of for a few days. Nancy has to stay horizontal for a couple days while things heal, and we have our small army of helpers (including Lulu, of course) already scheduled to ensure she's taken care of. Speaking of our adopted cat, Lulu is lying on Nancy's bed, front paw over her leg, purring loudly and exercising her mysterious feline curative powers, which seem to be more effective than much of what we experience in the ER.

So there's the rather uninteresting story. I said to Nancy—there's always '08. I hope we didn't cause any unnecessary consternation with the sudden change of plans, and I was glad to hear from Helen that the party was a success. We are both really sorry to have missed it.

I hesitate to predict the future, but with that caveat, I look forward to seeing you on Monday.

—Rick

December 22, 2007
(My family spent the holidays in Florida.)

Dear Rick,

How thoughtful of you to remember Carol's birthday in the midst of everything else you have going on. There is a viable address here but then it goes to the rental office and I think it's safer to send it home where the dog sitter is taking in her mail. Also she'll need the money when she gets home. This will buffer the reality of coming home from vacation broke. Sorry Nancy has all this raw skin. It hurts like hell and looks awful. I hope the swimming makes it feel better. I hope the two of you can have a wonderful quiet weekend. You both need it.

Love, Mother

Okay, Carol's gift will be there when she gets home.

I'm going on a swimming blitz today through Monday—no outdoor pools around here are open every day so swimming opportunities are scarce during the holidays. Hope to drag Nancy to the pool today—she wouldn't go yesterday—too tired. Sometimes I feel like my older brother, pushing her, but she needs to get back in gear.

The script she is following is so similar to what Lance Armstrong went through, it's scary. And I say that *not* being a big Lance fan. All you need to do is read his first book. It's not about the bike—the denial, diagnosis, brush with dying, finding out after a year of treatment that one of the tumors was in fact dead, then a long period of depression and listlessness dealing with symptoms that won't go away. Well, Lance went on to win the Tour, and I'm hoping with patience and gentle prodding, Nancy might win her own Tour in some way.

—Rick

February 14, 2008
Not a good day for Nancy today—they each have their complexions. Nephrologist/urologist today—getting her to the office and doing everything and getting her back is hard on her. Her mental state is, of course, one of anxiety, and she's adjusting to some major changes in drugs, which upsets her digestive track from top to bottom. In a few days I think we'll get it all straightened out, but meanwhile, you can accumulate a lot of wisdom, but it doesn't make you feel better right now.

Nancy starts on antibiotic (Cipro-like) tomorrow to get ready for her outpatient surgery on Tuesday, and the Oxy finally came in. Hopefully both will help—she may have a minor urinary tract infection, so the antibiotic may have a good side-benefit besides prep for the procedure. I just hope things get no worse—ER visits we don't need. She's asleep now.

Frankly, I understand I will have to be one of the people who escorts Nancy through a very tough experience to its end. I think I can handle that, more or less. But watching her break down with the news, which I think she already had intuited, and the sound of it in a doctor's office at 6:00 p.m. on a dim winter's evening, I doubt I'll get over that any time soon. I've never felt more badly for a person. It's so hard to just watch and be helpless.

I guess she's feeling best if she's just left alone for a while. She is trying to come to grips with all this. I'm computing from her bedside, present but otherwise occupied, for moral support. Let's give it some time and see where she gets to emotionally after a few days go by. It's pretty raw at the moment, and I can't blame her for that. She's overwhelmed.

February 15, 2008

I guess what's happened is Nancy's primary care is now in-home hospice, with the oncologists as backup.

I spoke with Tom tonight. He's the great agitator for doing more more more, and I asked him—should we be doing more? He's recommending that only if we would get some peace of mind with another opinion. Nancy is against trekking around town for opinions.

The options are to find some magic bullet cure, and that's highly unlikely, or to intervene—i.e., with surgery—to decrease the tumor size, which would be sort of a stopgap. Tom's not recommending either. The magic bullet is unlikely to exist, and his experience with people who try to help these situations with surgery is that surgery makes things worse, especially in the sensitive region where Nancy's got this problem. However, Tom is talking with the surgeon Nancy has worked with to get his opinion.

Nancy is fine with me doing telephone research, but she's not desperate to do more. Her stated goal is to be comfortable and spend what time she can enjoying what she can from home. She's pretty content to have me here for company, the TV, computer, the cat, and her phones. That's the "bargain" in the speak of this business.

Her hospice MD calls every day and is coming on Monday to audit her meds and help her stabilize on the pain med— Oxycodone. Tom is watching him, too, and knows him, and says he's doing exactly what Tom would do. It's nice to have that second opinion a phone call away.

Nancy and I discuss the bigger picture only for a few minutes per day. Who could handle any more than that? To her credit, she's a realist, and I think knew a while ago this is where things were headed. She says she knew the tumor was growing, but like Lance, preferred to extend the bliss of ignorance via denial and focus for a while on physical therapy and wound care. At least the wound is not bothering her, and she's in a good mood overall, with minimal pain, if any. I think there's a certain peace to any decision, and for the moment, she's okay with things. I mean this is not where anyone would want to be, but you know what I mean.

—Rick

Dear Rick,

If there were a magic bullet to take the nightmare away I would say go for it but, I agree with Nancy. She is too tired to fight anymore, and she just wants to be left alone with her limited energy and medicines. I said before that I admire her acceptance. She is a great person. Trust her and allow her to be captain of her fate. I know this is tough on a person who is active and is used to solving all problems. But my feelings are trust Nancy. Daddy and I are with you and Nancy and will do anything for you. Just say the word.

Love, Mother

February 15, 2008
(from a memo to the executive staff of AeroAstro)

I had a discussion with our CTO, Bill, yesterday, and, while somewhat personal, I want you all up to speed since Nancy's situation is going to make some accommodations by me a good idea.

In the last 14 years, Nancy and I have kept things under control by a series of tricks, and when each trick stopped working—various surgeries, radiation, drugs, chemo (there are lots of variations on each)—we moved on to the next. But the duration of relief has shortened, and our latest gambit has now stopped working for her.

Nancy's got really no good treatment options, and her care has switched to maintenance of quality of life for as long as possible. Her primary care is now coming from a hospice center MD whom we've been working with for a month now as a complement to oncology. But now oncology is secondary, and hospice is becoming primary.

We have no idea how long this period would be—weeks, months, a year, or even several years. We'll know more as we watch how things progress. It is impossible to know. If there's one thing the medical community has learned about patients with situations like Nancy's, it's that no prediction is possible, especially in her case where the disease is so rare—it's tantamount to predicting the life span of one of our experimental miniature satellites.

While there's still a possibility of entering a protocol at Georgetown, it's not clear that would change what now seems to be the likely progression of things. Sometimes miracles happen, but the motivation to do a new protocol is more to support scientific progress than to bank on a cure. On the other hand, some patients do well for a long time after the serious cancer treatments end, since the treatments themselves are so difficult.

It's tragic news, but we have had years to prepare for this eventuality. It's not a surprise, and while we've hoped for the best, we have done our best to prepare for this possibility.

I am not ready to make any general pronouncements—I want to get used to things myself and ensure this diagnosis is stable and reliable. I'd like to wait a week or two at least before talking with the company or with Radyne. I'll call our new CEO once I think I can articulate myself clearly. People not experienced with this sort of thing tend to not understand what's going on and what it means. Bill asked if I wanted to do a sabbatical. Nancy and I had talked about it, but we both agreed that's the opposite of what we'd like. I prefer to work as close to normal as possible and to exercise the flexibility necessary to accommodate the day-to-day exigencies, with no set time horizon on when things might change one way or another.

During this interim period, I'm planning to work as a remote from Reston, not that there's any more to do at home with her care than usual—maybe less. There are plenty of people available to do those things, but I just want to be close by for moral support. In the old days I managed to be remote for a few weeks from Europe or Japan or Rhode Island or Bob's apartment in San Francisco. Reston remoting should be easy since I can get to the office when necessary and do DC briefings with our lobbyists. But when I don't have a reason to be somewhere, I plan to be working from home.

I would appreciate your working with me to understand that there may be interruptions to my keeping an occasional appointment. I also would welcome suggestions re how to handle the staff when we decide to tell them. Nancy and I don't want people to be alarmed. After so many years as a cancer patient, Nancy has learned that while we have come to accept what's happening to her, it's a disturbing topic for others. We don't want to upset people or create some feeling that people need to do something for her. Plus, as poor as the outlook is this week, for all we know we could go through another long quiescent period, as she had for most of the three years she worked at AeroAstro. I don't want to essentially tell people we're in an end game and then have that turn out to be false.

So why am I mentioning this at all? I want you to know that I'm working remotely and why and get your help in managing any impact on the rest of the AeroAstro staff and operations. My one fear in divulging more information is that someone will call Nancy. She does not want to start advertising her situation, at least until she understands it better.

Thanks in advance, and my apologies if I'm upsetting anyone. My intent is the opposite. This isn't the outcome anyone wants, but it happens, and as well as we can, we're accepting that's the way things will be.

—Rick

February 16, 2008
Nancy's much healthier today. As the Tarceva wears off, she's almost able to sit up. Her appetite and thirst are back to normal for the first time in months.

We talked for a long time, more than an hour. She's more optimistic now. I think the switch from her older painkillers to Oxy, which is a sort of a Vicodan without Tylenol, is also helping. My suggestion, which she agreed with, is we are going to do a test and return to using Tarceva every other day since it does seem to slow the tumor growth and buys some time for her. Taking it every other day seems to not hurt her. Every day was an overdose and didn't help anyway, as the latest images show. But a slow-growing tumor is not tantamount to death. The slower it grows, the longer one can do things. Many men live with that in their prostate. It will kill eventually, maybe in a year or maybe in ten. In Nancy's case, the time scale may be shorter, but one never knows. We all have physical faults—bad knees, bad shoulders, gout, missing fingers, or even limbs—whatever. She has a growth somewhere in there, but if it's not stopping her from doing anything, and it does not have a proclivity to go other places (unlike Lance's), it makes no short-term difference.

Our conclusion is, had she been healthy, she would have

worked another ten or fifteen years at frustrating jobs (as you did), hoping to save enough to retire. As it is, she's getting paid to retire right now and, thanks to insurance, gets to skip the fifteen additional laborious years. So it's time to retire and enjoy what's left of life. Nancy wants to feel good enough to get out of bed and maybe go to Rhode Island. She's had it with doctors and the idea of being tied to Reston and Fairfax hospitals to be close to the oncologists, the surgeons, radiology, nephrology, nurse practitioners, etc. That's over. They have nothing to offer her anymore. She has what she has.

I have to admit her attitude is remarkable. I'm game for anything she wants to do. This week we have to take on this kidney thing, which is an outpatient operation on Tuesday to protect a kidney from being blocked by the bulk of the tumor. Assuming that goes ok, and Tom is confident it will, a week later may be time to try a short ride in her car. She's anxious to at least be a passenger in her beloved Beetle. Just the desire to do anything is a major change.

It's very odd, but the declaration that she has a condition that cannot be treated, only ameliorated, and is eventually fatal, has freed Nanct from the system. I'm sure you can appreciate. It's like a painting where the colors are underneath a covering of black. You can occasionally scratch the black and see some colors come through. It's a nice relief, and I'm glad for her. There's an overlay of tragedy, but at least a few breaks in the overcast for now.

—Rick

February 19, 2008
Nancy is one hundred percent comfortable now. The Tarceva has worn off, and the wound is healed. The Oxycodone is

working fine. She still has plenty of pain sites from the tumor, and I don't really understand what else. But the Oxy is covering fine. She even slept through the night last night. It is the best I've seen her sleep in months. No doubt another shoe will drop, but we're enjoying a respite today.

I had a long talk with our nurse/neighbor, Susan, who was walking her huge dog, a labradoodle. Susan's mom was cared for in the same office as Nancy. Like Nancy, they worked with her, but when the treatment didn't work, they turned her over to hospice and, like Nancy, her mom had a feeling she was being set out on an iceberg to die. I don't fully blame the doctor for that. It's today's medicine. They all specialize in disease and treatment, and if you don't have their disease or work with their treatment, they pass you off to the next pair of hands in the assembly line. Nobody at Ford builds a car. They just weld or paint or screw fenders on.

Nancy was depressed over her treatment, but I think, via Susan's experience, she can distance from that. She has many people who do care for her—all of us in the family, Susan, Tom, and her hospice MD. That's better than average.

While I don't want to become a nut always thinking there's a magic bullet behind door number three, I'm not completely turning this over to fate. Susan and I agree the Tarceva might have a benefit at half-dose. Nancy is tolerating that fine, whereas full strength was worse than the disease. At worst, the Tarceva will do nothing. Possibly it will buy some time. It's not a cure. Psychologically, it's much better than doing nothing. Hope is important.

One way to think of Nancy's disease is like prostate cancer.

It's not curable, but not necessarily rapidly fatal either. But as the tumor grows, it creates pain and dislocates other organs. Hence, the operation Tuesday to protect her kidney. That's also why she's taking Zometa monthly—to protect the hip. I've asked Tom to talk with her surgeon about "debulking," which amounts to something like tumor liposuction. If it can be done via a needle/keyhole, we might do it. If it's real surgery, that's out for many good reasons.

In any case, we're trying to enjoy our "retirement." We watch movies and eat sushi from our home hospital bed. Under the circumstances, things could be worse. If we can salvage some peaceful time for Nancy now, we've accomplished what none of the physicians could, among whom I exclude Tom, who's been on her side all the way. Like thermodynamics, it's all about where you draw the boundaries. If you expect physicians to perform outside of their boundaries, you'll be disappointed, because a pretty big part of this game isn't inside anybody's boundary.

—Rick

February 21, 2008

Nancy's recovering from the long day yesterday, when the kidney drain was installed. Now, on top of her other problems, she has the drain, the dressing, and the external bag. Plus, she's exhausted and a little sore. We left the house at 8:30 a.m. Tuesday and got home at 5:30 p.m. It was more than full workday for her.

Her favorite MD visited today and brought up the topic of hospice care. Nancy didn't want to hear that, but she did feel it was appropriate. He knows how to handle that discussion, explaining that hospice is not a decision that life is ending. It's a system that allows them to assign a small team to Nancy led by a hospice nurse, who would authorize doctor visits, all Nancy's pain meds, and physical therapy. Home health care and even social work is all covered under their umbrella. He told me later hospice such a good program that they have to force people out of it when it's not appropriate. It's one of the few places in health care where they focus on the patient, not the disease or procedure.

I think his advice was good advice, and he sincerely offered it to get Nancy better care. He spoke with me for a while after his visit. He's a genuine guy, and he knows the biggest obstacle to better care for Nancy is if she resists the hospice label. But she's okay with it. She was depressed at first, but it appeals to her realistic side, and also she agrees it's a better deal for the patient. Nobody had to convince her of anything.

So we'll have a visit from the hospice nurse to get her started. Then I spent a few hours (literally) chasing down medications. I was about eighty percent successful—one can never hit one hundred percent, thus every trip eventually results in another trip. By the end of the month, you hit a hundred percent, but then the counter resets to zero again. That's if there are no changes, and there are always changes. Maybe they have a hospice pharmacy.

Nancy is somewhat more uncomfortable now that she can only lie on one side, thanks to her new access port. But she's sleeping and resting comfortably. I hope tomorrow the access port side is a little less tender. If it isn't one thing, it's another.

—Rick

Rebecca

Courtesy David Ascalon of Ascalon Studios

February 25, 2008

Maybe I've gone a little too long in carrying out my pledge not to clog your inbox with updates on Nancy. But assessing her and her prognosis is a moving target, which makes sending out a simple status report difficult.

Our present situation is that, despite some temporary gains, none of her treatment options, conventional or experimental, have provided a lasting attenuation of the disease. Nancy's been more than heroic in what she's been willing to put herself through, but at this point we've run out of silver or any other material bullets for treatment. Her disease is being left to follow its course, a strategy that probably works better for colds and flu, but it's what we're left with. Living with the disease is nobody's first choice, but it has its upsides. Nancy is not suffering the effects of radiation, chemo, surgeries, and toxic drugs. She's comfortable and we have the opportunity to spend time together at home and not in a hospital.

Nancy is receiving hospice care here at our house in Reston.

This does not mean we feel the end is very near, but it does mean that her care is now focused on the palliative. She is young, generally healthy, and strong, so this phase could last a long time. Despite his age and poor condition, Art Buchwald spent years in hospice. He wrote a book about it and appeared on every radio talk show in sight (ok, he did not make it onto Rush). Every treatment option has its probability of efficacy and its expected value for length of life worth living, including this one. Our focus is on quality over quantity, since we can effect the former, and nobody can predict or change the latter.

Our plan now is to do our best to enjoy Nancy's early retirement. For now, while her pain is well-controlled without too much medication, enjoying her time is actually possible, though Nancy is pretty much confined to bed. She consumes several books per week and keeps Netflix order-fulfillment people hopping.

Our philosophy is to not cling to hope as a way to avoid dealing with the realities of the situation. However, at the same time, we keep the door open to, if not a miraculous recovery, an extended period with each other. Nancy and I can enjoy being together and spending time with family. The rebuild of our house in Rhode Island will be completed mid-March, and we are not ruling out the possibility of visiting it later in the spring. Nancy's sisters and mother and my parents visit regularly and have been a tremendous help to her and to me. We also have an excellent complement of caregivers with my brother, Tom, serving as our Vice President of Common Sense (a commodity as rare in medicine as it is in business).

I realize this all sounds pretty serious, because it is serious.

But Nancy and I have had adequate time and experience with her disease to accommodate ourselves to the reality, and we are focused on the life we have now, not some fictional life we thought we deserved or hope to have in the future. I don't want to gloss over what we're experiencing. It's not what we expected or what anyone would want to contemplate. But there are, even in difficult times, some positives, and we are drawing upon those when we can. There are some tough episodes, but overall Nancy feels the best she has in months, and we're spending a lot of enjoyable time together.

Lulu continues to be a great companion for both of us. This is where a good cat can really shine, and she's doing well in the spotlight. Nancy's primary care nurse calls her our "healing cat." She sits beside Nancy, a miniature sphinx, for long stretches when Nancy is unable to really move, and rests a paw on Nancy's hand. So far Lulu has done as much good, and far less harm, than at least some of the stuff we've tried.

Nancy occasionally has to be in the hospital for treatments to control the various peripheral effects of the disease, and those interventions definitely provide her more time and significant relief. Lulu is a great care adjunct, but I wouldn't trade in Nancy's medical team for a small cat. We just are lucky to have a complete and excellent team behind her, one of whom happens to pad around the house on four white paws.

As for doing something with or for Nancy, my advice remains about the same as always—cards. She rarely talks on the phone, and visitors are even rarer, given her extremely low energy level. You can, on the other hand, bug me at any time via this email address or my cell phone.

Thanks for your caring. I'll send more news when I have it.

—Rick

February 26, 2008

The "procedure" went perfectly today. Nancy has a brand new stent and things seem to be flowing from both her kidneys. She still has the drain from her kidney to the outside. The surgeries produce a lot of gunk the surgeon doesn't want to let filter through the kidney, thus it's draining into her external bag. But tomorrow we can take the bag off and cap the drain tube. Then they leave the line in for a week just in case a problem occurs. It's traumatic to put a line in and almost impossible to put in a second one, so they want to be sure all is well before removing that link. It is all medical mechanics none of us really understand.

Nancy's hospice case nurse is coming tomorrow at 9:30 a.m. and will take off the bag. She will put the stub of the line under a waterproof dressing, and that will allow Nancy to shower. Nancy is like a ballet dancer, which means she's like a cat and doesn't care much for showers anyway. I've been cleaning her with a washcloth and that's fine with her. But I think a shower will be a nice change—it's been nine days! I think she partly is shying away from the shower because of the effort.

I have two shifts of volunteers coming in just to be here. One from 10:30 to noon, and another from 1:30 to 4:00. We have the exact same schedule on Thursday, since I have to be gone nine to five both days. Tomorrow our nurse/neighbor is also coming by, so Nancy will have more than enough companionship for the eight hours.

We have her meds pretty straight, and she's more comfortable now. I think she's benefitting from the stent already—she's more comfortable even with the line still in.

Hospice delivered a whole oxygen setup yesterday. I assume they want it on hand just in case. Very nice technology. It has a cooler and makes its own oxygen by distillation out of ambient air. No tanks. Then they lugged in four tanks "in case of a power failure." Yikes. These people are intense.

I'm trying to get Nancy's old bed picked up so that hospice can install a fancier one with air cushioning the patient can adjust. Tom says cancer is hard on skin, and they are ever-vigilant about bedsores.

Nancy's comfortable, but a little out of it due to all the meds today. We'll be back at Reston hospital next Tuesday, when they'll withdraw the drain. Then this phase is over. I'm thankful for that. That's the day before her sister Karen arrives, so all should be back to normal by then.

—Rick

February 27, 2008

Mom, per our conversation yesterday on what you and Dad can bring/do. Here's my semi-profound thought du jour.

The best thing you can do is stay healthy. I can handle only one major loss right now. I am supported in doing that by ignoring that it won't be the only loss, though likely will be the first. Unlike most people my age, this is all new to me, and, selfish as it is, I want to believe the rest of my network is going to be there for the foreseeable future.

I actually believe the same is true for Nancy. As long as there are no other crises, she can be the focus, and that's helpful to her—that we're focused on her well-being. As you say, available when she wants, fade away when she wants solitude. Another family crisis would compromise our flexibility for her. We can handle that. We're strong people in our family and we tend to handle whatever comes at us, but if we're talking about what's the best we can do for her and for me, for you to stay healthy is the best thing I can come up with.

I know it's the thing nobody has much control over. But I've found, in my proclivity for breaking my own bones, as with our favorite chef's car accidents, that simply paying a little bit more attention to not getting in accidents actually helps. That would be my Number One request.

I hope this doesn't come off as totally ridiculous. Maybe with all your experiences, you know what I mean.

—Rick

March 1, 2008
Not to be totally Teutonic negative about things, there are some good reasons to soldier on here:

1) Nancy's being sick tends to make us focus on the trees. The oozing wound, pain, difficulty walking, her bodily functions, lack of appetite, and not much hair—all of which are pretty real. That's where your mind goes. Since I'm not suffering firsthand, I can think about the forest, which is, for all we know, just left over symptoms of a lot of toxic treatment and side effects of her surgeries. She has had two of them in the last ten days. Nobody would feel their best at this point.

So I feel like my job is to cheerlead this process. It's possible we can recover from these many little obstacles and come out the other end with a period of relative good health. People live well with various cancers for many years when the treatments or side effects aren't dominating things.

2) Even if the trees are all there, what's the right thing to do? At the end of any experience, either in college, with a company, or in this one, we'd like to be able to say we did our best to get a positive outcome. The outcome will be what it is, and we have limited control over it. How we perform to help a person is one-hundred percent controllable, within human limits. That's where I am—whatever happens, I'm going to wake up the next morning and say I couldn't have done any better for her in the big picture. That doesn't mean I'll run off to Kuala Lumpur and Mexico looking for peach-pit cancer cures. It might mean doing my best to not force her to do things she can't contemplate doing, and improving her situation within her scope of possibilities—pushing the envelope but not tearing it. It doesn't mean I won't go to the pool and ride the bike; those things help me to be at my best for this whole challenge.

3) In the bigger picture, nothing is forever. Let's not get too focused on a day or two of pain. Athletes work for years just for a chance to compete—and usually not win. There's nothing so heroic about our situation. We're doing what people do: putting in a lot of blood, sweat, and tears for an uncertain outcome. That's the nature of things for people everywhere. It's not a guarantee, but it's a way to make being lucky more likely.

—Rick

March 1, 2008

Since things have been so bad, I thought I'd give some updated better news.

Nancy was a little more with it tonight, having pretty much slept all day minus a few minutes here and there. The medication and the disease combined are a big load on a person, plus the anxieties as we discussed. We talked about her eating, and she recognizes the problem and said that the meds suppress her appetite, and the MD said that would subside as she adapts to the Oxy. Tonight she really seemed to be working with me to find a few things she could handle. Plus I'm going with your attitude, which is that food is one area where she has a little control and I should just help her to go where she wants in that regard.

When she's a little better, she doesn't seem headed away from life, and that's the reason to keep trying. It's impossible to know where all this will go and on what schedule. Now she's watching a Woody Allen DVD.

—Rick

March 2, 2008

Nancy is having a much better day today.

She got me up at the usual 1:00 a.m. time for an ice refill, but otherwise slept well through the night. The dressing and drain remained pretty dry, and no dressing change was needed.

She was pretty groggy this morning and still experiencing weird dreams, but less so. I made a small breakfast per her requests, which she touched none of.

Tom visited and said she looked improved. I thought so, too. Her body is functioning better, and she's more relaxed. Tom, Alan. and I went out on bikes and Nancy's dance friend, Sheila, came by for an hour. Nancy had some anxiety about that, but she said later she was glad to have had the opportunity. Nancy then slept for the next three or four hours. The visit completely drained her.

This evening she actually had half a cup of matzo ball soup and some See's chocolate, a few nibbles on a tortilla, and the usual ice and Diet Coke. The more I work with her on diet, the more I understand. What to us seems ridiculous actually works for her. Nancy has a good sense of what she needs and what her system can handle. Except for my prodding her to intake more liquids, I think her self-regulation is fine at this point.

After several days of not handling even the computer, she watched a couple of movies today, and we talked about others I'd like to see. She read some emails, read *The Economist* and the NY *Times* (Style section only). She has only minor pain, mostly when she changes position and has to roll all the way around, or when getting out of bed and back in. But at rest, she's one-hundred percent comfortable. That's a huge relief— to be able to be comfortable. I know we've all been in situations where we couldn't even do that, and it's terrible.

So she's settling into the drug regime, and its agreeing with her. Even she said tonight that now that she's not hurting; she feels stronger. We're at a point where

no pain + no medical crises = A+.

We take what we can get around here.

It's too bad there's another small surgery Tuesday, but it will be the least trauma of the three so far, and we have tomorrow in peace. I'm sure Wednesday will be another recovery day and probably Thursday too. Nancy knows we're in for another tough week, but she's no whiner, that's for sure.

—Rick

March 7, 2008
Nancy improves daily post-surgery. Following my grandfather's advice: stay out of hospitals.

She is on pretty heavy doses of Oxy, but that's really all she takes now for pain. She's comfortable ninety-five percent of the time. She has spent several hours each day reading (mostly *People* magazine) and gabbing with Karen. The rest of the time she's asleep or watching a movie on her Mac.

I have the feeling this phase could last for a while. I have been trying to get a message through to Nancy that we are not leaving her to "die of cancer" (her words). There are many people alive today who only recovered after the doctors left them alone. Nancy was a healthy person when she walked into the oncologist's office last July and hasn't been since. She does have a serious disease, but that does not mean death is imminent. The point of all this is to nurse her back to health. Maybe it won't work, but that's the goal.

I don't know if she's fully buying it. I'm probably not fully buying it either, but what alternative philosophy is there? Nancy is a pragmatic realist. She knows how bad things look, but she agrees that the only logical approach is to try to get better and do more.

Anyway, it's just the last two days we have been able to have that conversation, even for two minutes. Previously she was too sick to do much more than exist. Anita, you know Nancy doesn't like to discuss big issues head-on. But she can sometimes accept it for a couple of minutes. She basically would prefer to change the subject, and I'm fine with that. No gain in dwelling on a disease.

Karen has been great. Nancy has really appreciated her visit. Mom comes Monday, but first on Sunday she has a visit from Ko, who worked for Nancy at American Ballet Theater. Next Friday, one of Nancy's close friends from the NYC Ballet world, a woman who taught the ABT dancers for decades and then was dismissed with no warning, is coming down for a quick visit. The next day, Anita, arrives with her sister, Jean.

So Nancy's social schedule is full, but hopefully not overly full. The trick, I think, is to just sit there and go with whatever energy level she has at each moment.

Not much more to report today. Lots of prescriptions to refill tomorrow. She now has a one-week pill box (mom knows this system well). It's a daunting schedule of drugs to remember, but Nancy and Karen have it all organized.

—Rick

March 16, 2008
Thought I'd write when not at end of my day.

Nancy had a big day on Friday with my mom and me here in the morning. Then her friend, Diana, from NYC was here for an hour, then the physical therapist's initial visit was in the early afternoon. She didn't eat much other than part of an orange and part of a Boost, but things were peaceful, and there were no problems.

Overnight was harder. She called at 11:30 for help, then at 12:30. Then I heard her voice at 2:00 a.m. Half asleep, plus with the effects of the drugs, Nancy missed the bed getting from the commode and was half-sitting, half-lying on the floor. Unhurt, but thoroughly confused, and of course she can't stand up. This is partly since her muscles have atrophied, partly because she has lost a lot of pelvic bone, and partly because the drugs make any exertion very difficult.

After about a half hour of body mechanics, my Red Cross swimming guard/life saver courses finally came in handy. They teach you how to get an unconscious person up and out of a pool. Only partly conscious, she advised I call 911 (that's always an option). But by the time the police show up, decide they can't do anything and call an ambulance, etc., you're talking all night messing with people and likely ending up in the hospital in an ambulance. Not just back in bed, which was all she really wanted. Together she and I got her on her knees by the bed, arms over the mattress. I pulled on her arms from the other side and gradually got her body up on the bed, whereupon she rolled so that her head ended up at the foot of the bed and her feet were at the head. So I remade the bed backwards, and all was peace with the world. She fell back asleep. I went to bed. Thirty minutes later she called for Karen. At first I thought it was a dream, but Nancy had forgotten that Karen wasn't here anymore, and she thought the heater was on (there's no heater in there). Typical Oxy hallucinatory dreaming.

I calmed her down. By now it's 300 a.m. I suggested we both get some sleep. In the morning, Nancy was awake and easily crawled into normal position on the bed. During the day today she's been fine again and doing everything like normal, as if nothing happened.

Why do I tell this whole story? So that Nancy's mom Anita gets a feel for how things go around here. It's all a little crazy, but you have to take it with a sort of sense of humor and not feed into Nancy's worries. None of these situations is particularly serious or life threatening, but it's easy to panic when Nancy panics. My advice is don't get excited. Calm her down and work through whatever the crisis du jour happens to be. Had she not gotten into bed, I would make her a "bed" on the floor. She's just too disoriented at night to get back into bed. In the morning she can do it. So at first I thought, just put a bunch of pillows on the floor, blankets, etc., and she'll do fine. I'll also leave you a variety of phone numbers. Hospice can have a nurse here in less than thirty minutes. That's your next best choice if you can't handle something on your own.

—Rick

Ruth and Naomi

March 25, 2008

I wondered how your experiment of leaving Nancy and her mother alone worked out? I think her mother probably just stays out of the way when you are around but when you're not there, she stays close to Nancy. Your mention of Nancy's weakness is probably a temporary symptom. Her symptoms do seem to change daily, and hopefully, she will be a little better tomorrow. These ups and downs are nerve-racking and common for someone in her condition. That said, it doesn't make it any easier to cope with. All you can do is hang in there and hope for the best.

—Dad

Dad,

The experiment went very well. It definitely gave Anita the chance to solo, and she rose to the occasion. So that was just the right move. We'll repeat it today and actually the rest of this week every day for a few hours. They both liked it. I call that a success.

The nurse and doctor, who are visiting again today, say the weakness is the normal progression of the disease. It will be up and down, but overall gradually down. Likely, Nancy will not be able to get out of bed again. We all discussed with Nancy and Anita, as is the style these days. Honesty can be brutal, and it was tearful all around. But now that the subject is breached, and Nancy realizes that is the way it is, she is wrapping her mind around it. Hard to do, and I'm glad the two pros handled it. They do this at least once per week with patients. I've never been in a room for that kind of discussion before.

Their time line for her now is "weeks to months." They can't be more specific. But this gives Nancy something to work with in terms of planning whom she wants to still see and other arrangements important to her. The mood is, I'd say, a mix of sadness and practicality, and the focus is one hundred percent on giving Nancy maximum choice on how to handle this. At Nancy's request, they are bringing a Do Not Resuscitate form tomorrow, so in case 911 comes, they won't intubate her and ship to an ER. She is also doing a living will.

As I've been saying, this is all surreal. You can't believe it's really happening, but it is, and you just have to get with the program. Your trip is excellent timing. I think you will find her realistic about what's going on and interested in talking at least a little bit. I just let her lead. Mostly, she'd rather talk news and about other things in the outside world, very rarely about herself or her condition. Tom and I, at her request, are working on getting a rabbi to visit. Not for religious reasons so much as to talk about what the Jewish perspective is on death. Again, I'm glad to have a pro handling that, despite however much reading I do. I'm expecting that visit late this week. I sit in on all this because Nancy likes to have me there, and it helps me to see what she's thinking.

—Rick

March 28, 2008
Something a little different for this update, a break from my usual litany of medical details and my amateur interpretations of them.

I welcome a few new people to the distribution list—late-coming but glad to add you to the ad hoc community.

Thoughts, cards, and interest in keeping up with Nancy's progression are a comfort to her, to me, and to our families. I read to Nancy every day the cards and emails I get for her. Each one is appreciated.

—Rick

The Life Cycle of Butterflies

My first and last biology class was in junior high school exactly forty years ago. Other than confirming my distaste for animals and lack of interest in plants, I also remember something about the life cycles of butterflies and moths. They evolve through four diverse stages, with the same individual taking on completely a different appearance and behavior with each passage. Finally, they graduate to the most beautiful stage, when as adults they show off their wings, flying precariously in summer sunshine over meadows and through deep green forests. I wished, as an overweight and socially clumsy thirteen-year-old, that I could hope for such a makeover sometime in my future, emerging into a life of physical beauty and freedom (from eighth-grade biology among other oppressions). I suppose my desire, the aesthetic appeal of these animals, and their freedom to fly aimlessly outdoors with no apparent destination or motivation other than to play, imprinted them, just a little, on my psyche.

But there is another reason my thirteen-year-old self was impressed by their story. It was not so much their designs, colors and flight as the dissonant tragedy that goes hand in hand with their hard-earned maturation, and with it, the freedom to fly. Some of the species, upon achieving their adult phase, can no longer eat. Each individual lives for only a few weeks or at most months, burning up fuel stored during earlier lives.

Apparently, the inevitability of their end doesn't inhibit them. Maybe it even motivates them to fascinate us, to brighten our world, and for the time that they have, to make more of living than without them we would ever know.

March 30, 2008

As you may know, Nancy has not eaten in about six days—excepting Diet Coke, a little cran-grape juice, and grape-flavored shaved ice.

Tonight she and Karen are watching a DVD, and Nancy asked for a turkey bologna sandwich. I put it together on her favorite white bread with a little mustard and cut it attractively into two diagonals and put it next to her in bed—not making a huge big deal. Nancy is a person who has been unable to even pick up her cell phone to call me for help. I offered to help her but she said she was fine by herself, and proceeded to eat twenty-five percent of it.

Now I don't take that to mean we've cured cancer here, but it does say something about the value of surrounding the patient with the right environment. I have to admit, with all the effort we've all put into making Nancy's experience in this phase the best it can be, including things like anguishing over managing her visits, it's exciting to get a minor breakthrough. It's not the nutrition—it's the idea that her attitude is healthy enough that she can actually, at least comfortably, munch just a tiny bit of food.

This is what they teach you in hospice books and in practice—that the patient thrives the best, not in intensive care with every medical gadget in the world supporting her body, but at home with real people spending real time and effort to connect with her personally and provide TLC.

Bob, a friend of mine, took on the same role I now have when he cared for his father, who died at the age of one hundred about ten years ago. Bob took a couple of months out of his own life for his dad's at-home hospice care, and he said it was one of the best experiences he ever had with his father. At the time, I thought it was a great way to rationalize the tragedy of death, but now I can understand what he was saying. Nancy is sometimes with it and sometimes not, but overall, she was happier today than I've seen her in the last six months.

—Rick

March 31, 2008
Karen and I spent most of the day with Nancy—along with Joan, her aide, and we had a visit from Colleen, her visiting nurse.

After a very "up" Sunday, we did a full body wash and bedding change. Nancy had thirty minutes of visitors (Sheila and Ned—her best friends from Maryland Ballet Company) and watched another long DVD with Karen. She even asked for and ate maybe ten percent of a bologna sandwich. Today was much quieter.

I had to pretty much wake her up for her 8:00 a.m. med, and then Joan and I changed her almost without waking her at 9:30. Tom came by, but Nancy was too tired to do much more than realize he was here.

By afternoon, she had slightly more energy, and talked with her nurse Colleen, who came by at her regular 4:00 p.m.

Nancy's vital signs and pain control are all excellent right now, and she had a good talk with Colleen and later with Karen and me. Colleen was really happy with Nancy's care and felt we had a good system in place—for now. And we have all the backup stuff at the house if anything changes. (In the hospice world, the word "changes" is a euphemism.)

After Karen and I spent some time with her, Nancy fell asleep again. Yesterday wore her out, but was well worth it. She is back to her accustomed eating habits—cran-grape juice, ice with a little cran-grape, and Diet Coke. I couldn't pin Colleen down on the time a patient can go on this way, but we did discuss that she is slowly getting thinner.

Well, nothing anybody can do about that, so we focus on a nice environment, good care, and catering to the patient. We're doing okay with that for now.

—Rick

April 1, 2008

After Joan got settled with Nancy, I took off for my usual bike ride—supposedly in the rain, but the forecast was wrong, and it was sunny and nearly seventy. No problems while I was gone, and I got the Joan debrief when I got back.

Joan is really good. She got Nancy cleaned, changed, and turned, and is happy that Nancy's pain control is one-hundred percent working. The problem now (and there's always something) is that her pain is worse, so her medication is more, and her lucidity time is going down. According to my reading, it's not just the pain med that causes this, but the disease itself that weakens her. Even if she didn't have cancer, on her diet one doesn't think as clearly without enough glucose in the system.

Tom came by later and suggested I give Nancy the Boost frosties I make—that she might not be able to tell the difference from her accustomed cran-grape ice. That worked sort of. In fifteen minutes of feeding, I managed to get maybe one-eighth of a bottle of Boost into her. Tom wasn't thinking this would be a breakthrough, but felt it might help her to at least get something in her other than water and diluted cranberry juice.

Her hospice MD is agreeing to our suggestion on the med change. Instead of 80 mg of Oxy three times per day and 15 mg six times per day (a total of 240 + 90 = 330 mg), we are going to 80 mg four times per day, and the 15 mg only as needed (320 mg plus as needed). About the same dose, but should be smoother—less medication peaks and valleys—and less clock-watching to do.

Tom showed Nancy some funny videos on YouTube and she seemed to enjoy them, but her state of consciousness today was only marginally better than Monday. She is seeing things that I'm not seeing, and she is not remembering much. These are all symptoms we've been experiencing for a long while, but they are just a little more pronounced the last day or two. I've read about all this in the medical and hospice literature, but it's one thing to read and another to experience. We're doing what we can, and the best I can say is she is comfortable and pretty happy. Karen's visit was a good one for her and I think well-timed.

Tomorrow is another day. My parents will be here from Wednesday evening to Sunday.

—Rick

April 4, 2008
To Karen and Anita

Sorry for the long lapse.

As you can imagine not much happens day-to-day. Nancy's nurse, Colleen, came by three afternoons this week, and her aide, Joan, was here all five days. My parents have been here since Wednesday, the day after Karen left, and are going back tomorrow. I admit I asked them to leave a day early for several reasons, primarily because Nancy wants a quieter house and no more houseguests. I think she mustered energy for you two and for Jean, and is exhausted. Houseguests create some commotion, and it was stressing her, so I suggested to my parents that there wasn't much they could do, and it was probably best to go home.

You can imagine I wasn't that comfortable asking, but I think they genuinely understood that Nancy doesn't want my attention divided and her need for quiet.

She is getting along well with Joan, who was a perfect find for Nancy. Nancy loves Colleen, as you both know. Since her two dance friends, Sheila and Ned, were here last weekend, she has not wanted to see anyone. Our housekeeper, Anita, is back from the Philippines, and I think she will fill Joan's role on Saturday and maybe Sunday. Anita has been handling Nancy since she became mildly disabled and they seem to have a quiet rapport. Nancy also is getting along well with Rabbi Steve and has been very focused on scheduling his visits. He will make his third visit Monday afternoon.

For now, that constitutes her circle—Anita, Joan, Colleen, Steve, and me. She's not even really interested in Lulu at this point. Having recently been with her, you understand her focus being narrowed commensurate with her decreasing energy.

There's a small skirmish now between Tom, who feels she should have an IV with fluids, and the hospice doc, who doesn't support that in these cases. Nancy and Colleen agreed to switch her to the morphine pump early next week so that it doesn't have to happen as an emergency. We hope it will be a smoother dosing with more control for her. She is now taking 80 mg Oxy five times per day plus three or four 15 mg short-term pills, so the low is 400 mg total. I think when Karen left, she was closer to 3 x 80 mg three times a day plus eight 15 mgs ... maybe around mid-300 mg. So we're definitely up another step, but plenty of room left to increase.

On the last visit Colleen reviewed with me how to use the oxygen system. Colleen's concern is that Nancy is fragile and could develop a need for the pump or oxygen at any time, and we should be prepared, so that's what we're doing. Nancy is fine with all that. She trusts Colleen, and that's enough reason right there. If Nancy takes some comfort in following her advice, it's good advice by definition.

So, overall, the slow decline continues. I don't think there's anything to do at this point. Nancy is comfortable and more and more wishing to be alone except for one person, me or Anita or Joan, sitting there twenty-four seven. Again, that's a wish we're all complying with.

I wish I could give you better news. Rabbi Steve tells me that Nancy expresses to him that she knows she is dying, and her associated fears, and that she understands how soon that could be. She does not mention any of that to me, and speaks with him in private. Like Colleen, Steve is coming more and more often. Colleen says that along with the narrowing of the circle, patients often segregate among different people, and it's not unusual to reserve the existential issues for clergy, only so as not to "trouble" the family.

Okay, that's enough for tonight. Don't hesitate to call or email if you want to discuss further.

—Rick

April 6, 2008
My parents left yesterday for the sunny climes of Cleveland. We had a nice spring day here yesterday, but it rained hard all night. Today it was drizzling and in the forties. Cleveland was sunny—amazing. Anita (the housekeeper, not the Nancy's folk-dancer mom) was okay with soloing with Nancy, so I went

out on the bike for a couple hours break. It was frigid and wet, but a good way to wake up.

However, the coldest spot in Virginia is in Nancy's room, since her medications raise her skin temperature and she likes the window wide open. I'm sitting with her feeding her cold drinks. She is wearing only a T-shirt. I'm in long pants, a sweater, and a winter jacket, and I'm still cold. I finally told Nancy I had to partly close the window since I wouldn't be much help to her with pneumonia. Even the cat has stopped coming into the room.

I learned a related fact from Bob Dylan's radio show today. Why is giving up morphine known as going "cold turkey"? Because morphine (same with heroin) causes your blood to circulate more at the surface of the skin, causing the skin warmth Nancy has had for weeks. Her MD and visiting nurse confirmed that it's normal with the drugs she is taking. If you suddenly give up morphine, the body strongly reacts the opposite way, putting no blood near the skin and surface. The skin turns icy cold and gets goose bumps, and a withdrawing patient's skin resembles a skinned turkey—cold, white, and bumpy.

The things you hear just by listening.

On to less happy news.

For whatever reason, Nancy's state of awareness is very low. I suppose this is partly because of the dose of pain med it takes to keep her comfortable, but she is changing even when the meds are not. She is still drinking, especially white peach tea (thanks, Mom!) and cran-grape. She managed two teaspoons of Boost today—not significant nutritionally, but something at least for variety. There have been a few times when I felt she had trouble swallowing, but not lately. She also had some labored breathing, but again, nothing notable today.

She barely talks. Mostly you ask a yes/no question and she nods, barely perceptibly. In addition, you have to time the question for when she is momentarily aware. If she does speak, your ear has to be right at her lips. A decoder ring would probably be a plus, too. A lot of what she tries to say is garbled.

Tomorrow her certified nursing assistant (CNA,) Joan, whom Nancy likes very much, comes at 9:30 to 2:30. She and her partner will both come. They plan to do a thorough cleaning and bed change. I clean Nancy top to bottom every day, but a bedding change takes two or three people. We did it Friday, so we're due. The rabbi, Steve, and Nancy's nurse practitioner, Colleen, are both coming in tomorrow afternoon. After the cleaning and change, I hope to taper down the pain med to maximize the chances she'll be able to converse with them. But if she starts to have pain, Joan and I will boost her back up.

She will not talk with me any more about visitors, so I'm asking the rabbi to bring it up with her. For now, I recommend against visiting. Yesterday she was very explicit—no more visitors. I understand her focus is narrow and her energy is zilch, but I'd like confirmation since I don't want to take the responsibility for gatekeeping unless I'm absolutely sure it's her desire. Colleen says, and my reading confirms, that some adult patients reach a point where they don't want to burden their family with seeing them in such a feeble state. Or maybe they just feel worse for the effort to see people. Or both. Anyway, it's normal.

But, another reason not to visit is, I don't know that there's much point unless Nancy becomes more conscious. Colleen will be starting up her medication pump tomorrow, and that may improve things a little, but I doubt it will make a material change.

Please email me with any questions. I hope this wasn't more detail than you really want to know. I'm trying to be sort of the next best thing to being there. I can say, bottom line, Nancy is not suffering, and her comfort is job number one. If we have to compromise between alertness and suppressing pain, there's no question. If she asks for the supplemental pain med, she gets it, and when she has the pump, she'll have the button so she won't even have to ask.

—Rick

April 7, 2008

The nurse and MD came today, and together we switched Nancy over to a morphine pump via her mediport. It's better in several ways, and she's definitely more comfortable and gets more control plus more immediate relief of transient pain, because now she has a "button" to get an extra IV dose on demand. She is definitely more relaxed and happier with this system.

She's still taking Boost, cran-grape, ice and peach tea, and, with Joan's suggestion, I made a sort of baby food of hot dog, potato, and beef bullion in the Cuisinart. Nancy managed a couple of teaspoons of that, too. She's had good and bad times today. The rabbi came late and she was too tired to see him, so he'll be back on Wednesday. At Nancy's request, she has a DNR notice posted—Do Not Resuscitate. Normal for patients like her—there is no point in extraordinary measures. So I signed that today and posted it as legally required.

This is truly an anguishing experience—more, of course, for her than for me. I remember when I had my first bike crash after moving to Southern California. Everything there is warm and sunny and green compared with Rhode Island and Cleveland, where the outdoors seems hard and unforgiving. Life just looks easier and brighter. But the southern California pavement, it turns out, is just as hard. Real life is like that—there are certain things that are there no matter what we do.

One bright spot is the great people taking care of Nancy. They really care. The nurse practitioner is coming almost every day now, and Joan is great. We are arranging for care over the weekend since this is beyond what I think Anita wants to take responsibility for on her own. Anita will be here to provide drinks, ice and handholding, but the CNA will handle the body cleaning and medication, and be there in case of emergency when I'm not here. I wouldn't feel good leaving Anita on her own. I don't feel that good leaving the house at all, but I'd probably feel even worse if I didn't.

Nancy reiterated to Colleen today that she doesn't want anyone to visit her. As I said the other day, this also is pretty much normal in these situations.

For me, I appreciate having all you out there, just to let you know what's going on. I'm available any time by email or phone if you want to talk further. Nowadays we go to bed at eight, and I get up at four. Nancy gets fully awake a couple of hours later. So other than those eight hours ...

—Rick

April 9, 2008

Nancy is quite near the end, the medical people tell me. She has not been eating for maybe ten days, and she doesn't drink much any more either. It's agonizing to watch her slip away from us, ever so gradually, physically and mentally. I just focus on doing the best I can for her every day.

Eventually, one realizes this is the nature of life. Maybe I'm fortunate to learn it before I became too set in a less realistic theory of what it's all about. This sort of experience teaches you a lot of humanity. I hope I can at least benefit from the education and somehow benefit others.

I don't mean to be overly frank or negative, but nature is what she is. As all long distance cyclists know, we can't change her—we can only bring appropriate clothing.

—Rick

April 9, 2008

Dear Rick,

Thank you for updating us on Nancy. I can't imagine what you're going through right now, but know that my thoughts and prayers are with you, Nancy, and your family right now.

—Mary Jo, a friend of Nancy's from ballet

April 10, 2008

We had a big day today with three nurses, plus me attending Nancy. The mission was to change all of her bedding down to the air mattress, get rid of the foam she had been on since

August and (the hard part) roll her onto her right side or at least her back. She has been lying on her left side for several months, and we all knew good things would not be happening to the skin supporting her.

We used up a lot of morphine in the process, but we did get it all done. Nancy and the bed are all fresh and clean. The whole room has been switched a hundred and eighty degrees. She can see all her flowers, computer, etc., now that she faces the other way. It took about two hours to do it.

She had several bad looking sores, but luckily none had broken through the skin, so we put various creams and ointments on all, but left her open to the air—still the best way to get fast healing. A dressed and lubrication-covered wound would heal with less possibility of scarring, but air-drying heals faster. Cosmetics are not high on our list these days.

I'm glad we did that. We couldn't have done it without Colleen, since she knew how much morphine to use. She is used to these procedures and directed the three of us.

Until then, Nancy had been having a good day, and we were joking around this morning. She watched one of her Netflix videos this morning while I got ready to go out. She wasn't one hundred percent with it, but had enough energy to stay awake and watch the video, and a couple of times I commented to her about it. Now I think it will be until Friday morning before she metabolizes all that painkiller, but at least she experienced no discomfort.

Karen and Anita, you should be prepared that Nancy is much thinner and hollower than when you saw her last. It is hard to see her and not feel just terrible at how cruel this disease is. I am providing her juice, ice, and Boost, which is all she'll take, whenever she'll take it, and as much as she can take, but the process is inexorable. How she remains sane through all this, I don't know, but she does. That is our miracle. I'm going to try chicken soup tomorrow to see if something salty appeals to her, but she's too tired now to play around with new things.

For some reason, we've migrated to an even earlier schedule. We now go to sleep about 8:00 p.m. I get up well before four, and Nancy's up maybe between five and six. Maybe it's natural to sleep when it's dark outside, and that's what she's responding to. It seems to work, and she sleeps soundly all night. I awake to check on her, and if she's awake I give her some of her three fluids to help her stay hydrated.

While she looks worse than when you saw her, she feels better. Pain is rare, her face and body are relaxed, and she's in a good mood. I thank hospice and the drugs for that—they really know what they're doing in that department.

I hope these emails at least help to keep everyone up to speed on the situation. They are not meant to alarm or depress anyone. As I'm always saying, it is what it is, and we do our best for her. Her medical team is the same way, and all of them have been nothing less than excellent. They're a real comfort to her and to me.

—Rick

Friday, April 11, 2008
(written before going to bed the evening of April 10)

I knew we didn't have much time, and facing what I knew would be a confluence of a personal crisis and a need to communicate best I could, I decided to write a first draft. Subconsciously, I believed I'd be revising this draft for many days, if not weeks. But this first draft became the final draft, which was sent out the next day.

Each of us receives a miracle every day—life. After fifty one and a half years, Nancy used up her store of those miracles today, ending fourteen years of living with cancer and the treatments that gave us that time. Nancy died in bed at home as she wished, with her cat, Lulu, oblivious as always, and her stuffed animals, including her spotted hound, Mr. Perkins, who was there even when I couldn't be, attending all her surgeries from inside a sterile plastic zip lock.

The last nine months, and especially the past nine weeks in hospice, gave both Nancy and me time to talk and to, if not accept, at least anticipate this end. Nancy faced the final phase of her life with the same acumen, balance, and realism she carried with her at work, in dance, and through her personal life. She never complained of her fate or her symptoms. Her major concern was the welfare of her friends, workmates, and family. I doubt I can ever attain her personal strength, but it was an inspiration to all of us who cared for her.

I will send another email about a memorial service, which will be in Herndon some time next week, and about opportunities to make a contribution in her memory once I get those details together. For now, I thank everyone on this list for their thoughts and support during our long and sometimes difficult mission.

I hope you will join me in keeping Nancy alive through our collective memories of her.

—Rick

Creation

Per Nancy's request, there will be a brief memorial service in her memory.

The Rabbi of Congregation Beth Emeth, Steve Glazer, was a great comfort to Nancy and has been a friend and spiritual guide to many of our family over the years. He will host the ceremony in the synagogue at 12523 Lawyers Road, Herndon, VA 21071. We will begin at 10:30 AM Wednesday, April 16.

A few people will make brief statements, and we will offer a traditional prayer. I anticipate the service will last no longer than an hour.

Please forward this invitation to anyone you think might wish to join the ceremony—I'm sure I have missed many in my distribution list.

For those few still managing without GPS, driving directions to Beth Emeth are at: http://www.bethemeth.org/directions.htm.

Nancy's only other stated wish regards gifts.

In the last years of her life, Nancy did *pro bono* work for Maryland Youth Ballet, where she managed its finances and was a member of its board of directors. On Nancy's birthday, in October 2007, the Maryland Youth Ballet Nancy Fleeter Costume Fund was established to celebrate Nancy's life, her love of dance, and her support of MYB.

Her wish was that donations be made to this fund, which has already enabled several costume overhauls in last winter's season performances. Alternatively, she hoped people would contribute to any charity with as much meaning to them as MYB has to her.

If you do elect to make a donation to her fund at MYB, it is 100% tax deductible as MYB is a registered 501(c)3 nonprofit. Donations may be sent to:

Maryland Youth Ballet
926 Ellsworth Drive
Silver Spring, MD 20910
Please specify The Nancy Fleeter Costume Fund
Receipts will be provided on request.

I look forward to seeing you on Wednesday.
—Rick

Messianic Age

NANCY FLEETER

On April 11, 2008, at her home in Reston, Va., with her husband, Rick Fleeter, by her side. Born October 18, 1956, in Los Angeles, Mrs. Fleeter is also survived by her mother, Anita Hartman, of Encino, CA, sisters Karen Hartman, of New Brunswick, NJ, and Jeanne Hartman of Los Angeles, and brother, Richard Hartman, of Sedgwick CO. Her late father, Sherman, was a thoracic surgeon in Los Angeles.

Mrs. Fleeter was devoted to ballet since age five, when she began her dance training. After earning her MBA at the University of Southern California, Nancy held a number of executive positions in major American fine arts organizations. Between 1989 and 1999, she served as Chief Financial Officer at The John F. Kennedy Center in Washington, DC. She later became CFO and then General Manager of the American Ballet Theater in Manhattan, returning to northern Virginia in 2004 as Chief Financial Officer of AeroAstro, of Ashburn, VA, a satellite-building firm she co-founded with her husband in 1988. She retired due to illness in 2007.

In the last three years of her life, Nancy did pro bono work for Maryland Youth Ballet, managing its finances and volunteering as a board member. Memorial donations may be sent to the Nancy Fleeter Costume Fund, Maryland Youth Ballet, 926 Ellsworth Drive, Silver Spring, MD 20910.

Friends and family will gather Wednesday, April 16 at 10:30 a.m. at Congregation Beth Emeth, 12523 Lawyers Road, Herndon, VA 21071.

April 14, 2008
To my close friend and cycling partner Alan

Subject: Today's Update

My father and I took the Colnago to the bike shop and had it reconfigured from Nancy's dimensions to mine.

Things get worse as time goes on. I am thinking Wednesday will be the low point. I always wondered if I could handle losing a parent, and now I'm facing something much harder, with a long crescendo that led up to the loss.

Reminds me of the Ironman competition. The marathon is hard enough, but the preceding two-mile swim and 112 mile bike ride sort of softens you up a little, making the marathon harder. Our swim started in 1993, the bike ride a few years later, maybe '99, when Nancy moved to NYC. My own marathon started on Friday.

I met with the Rabbi today and he reminded me of the Psalm segment, "Though I walk through the valley of death, I do not fear, for Thou art with me" (quote not exact—my memory). Having been through this, my regret of another loss will be no less, but my fear of it will never be as great. So there's something.

In the lingo of hospice, I am processing and learning, but learning is painful—almost always. A famous psychologist said that it is possible to have pain without learning, but not learning without pain.

—Rick

April 14, 2008
Rick,

I will look forward to the first Team Colnago ride.

Rick, it's hard to imagine what it is like for you to go through this. I lost both of my parents. That was very difficult. I felt very alone after my Mom died. But that was different. Although they were a huge part of my childhood, they didn't play a very big role in life after grad school. Nancy was very much your life partner. It must feel like you have lost a large part of yourself. I have said this before, but it is worth repeating ... your internal strength amazes me. I really admire your reply (before Nancy's death) to the, "Isn't this hard for you?" question. You said, approximately, "No, this is hard for Nancy. I'm supporting her." That was selfless, and an expression of your great love for your wife. Unfortunately, now, my friend, Nancy is gone and so you have a different answer to that question.

You have a great support structure: your parents, your brother. But when it comes down to it, it will be your own strength that gets you through this—gets you past Wednesday. Rick, how do you feel about company for a couple of hours tomorrow afternoon? About three o'clock or so? I have a few distracting stories. If you are overwhelmed with company as it is, no problem, I'll see you Wednesday.

Just to confirm, Nikki and I plan to attend the service together, but then she needs to get back to work. My plan is to go with the Fleeters back to Tom's. And then head out to the Leesburg airport (time permitting) with your Dad. Let me know about tomorrow.

—Alan

Alan,

This email deserves a little longer response—suggest working that with Team Colnago on Friday morning—sort of a one-week anniversary event? Watermelon not required this time.

You are right, today is way too booked, so let's meet up on Friday. You are doing me a great service by taking my dad up in your plane for an hour. He's a great guy, and I feel badly that he's made so many long trips here and I've not been much of a host. Not that he expects otherwise. I think being with you might give him a better window into me than being with me. And he just loves to fly.

I've learned many things. One that it takes a lot of something— mojo to stick with someone when they're on the rocks for whatever reason. You've been able to hang in there when very few have.

The airplane gadget will be therapeutic for my dad. The Colnago gadget did a lot for me. I guess it's true that men are all boys— our best feature.

—Rick

Letter from David
(David is a friend and employee from AeroAstro.)

Rick,

You haven't seen anything from me. I guess I've been holding off and letting you have the time.

Let me please relate my deepest condolences to you and to your family on your loss. I know having the time to prepare for it doesn't mitigate the reality of it happening, and my heart and JoJo's reach out to you. You have been in our thoughts this weekend.

I booked a ticket over the weekend, and I plan on being at the memorial on Wednesday. Don't worry. This is no inconvenience of any sort. It's something I very much want to do.

For what it's worth, we used the planned parley on Friday to reflect on Nancy and on the events of the day. We cancelled the business part of it, which everyone thought was a very appropriate thing to do, and had a moment of silence to reflect on Nancy and on our own blessings in our lives.

I also read two short quotes:

He who has gone, so we but cherish his memory, abides with us, more potent, nay, more present than the living man. ~Antoine de Saint-Exupery

If my doctor told me I had only six minutes to live, I wouldn't brood. I'd type a little faster. ~Isaac Asimov

I thought Nancy would appreciate the second one especially.

Let me know if there's anything JoJo and I can do for you in this time. My thoughts are with you.

Warmest regards,

David

Noah and the Flood

Memorial **Speech**

The guy who wrote those thoughtful and polished emails ... a disappointment in real life? Probably—I should be here to canonize if not deify Nancy, describe a heroic struggle against villain cancer, and finish with bitter grief and an overcast of mourning.

Maybe just a little—but first a few stories.

Let's not talk about our first date. Neither disaster nor epiphany, it was a miss—the friends who invited me to a concert with them forget to tell me I was having a blind date. I thought Nancy was their babysitter until she joined us in the car to head to Hollywood Bowl. After that, several weeks of unsuccessful attempts to connect. Second date, we used her free tickets to the Hollywood Bowl and were having too much fun to go home. On the other hand, too prudish to do what a young LA couple would do, so we drove to her apartment to pick up some jeans. While she rummaged and changed, I inspected the fridge—Diet Coke—and the cupboards—Sunshine, Hydrox, and Oreos. Then we drove to my apartment, where I also put on jeans. By now it was 2:00 a.m., and we drove toward the full moon up Highway 101 to Santa Barbara and Isla Vista for breakfast. We walked the University of California, Santa Barbara campus until the stores opened, then shopped for nothing in particular. It got to be afternoon and time to head back to LA. Both hungry, we ducked into a small grocery store and split up to pursue our prey. Meeting in the checkout line, Nancy had a cup of cheap black coffee and a package of Oreos. Me? A diet 7Up and three carrots.

Fast forward twenty-six-point-five years to April 10, the day before Nancy died. Joan, her day nurse, is getting ready to leave, finishing massaging Nancy's feet and legs, and I'm easing half-baby-spoonfuls of my special concoction between Nancy's chapped and bruised lips. It's a blend of ice, unsweetened cocoa, sugar, and a chocolate-flavored nutrition supplement the docs recommend for patients who can barely manage food. Nancy motions with her eyes for us to put our ears close to her lips. We both listen intently as she whispers—her last words to us? "First I ate a solid diet, then liquid, then ice. Now it's the frozen Oreo diet. " She smiles the biggest smile I've seen in weeks. We all have a big laugh, and Joan leaves, planning a good day coming. She tells me in her Trinidadian lilt, as we walk to her old Buick, "Nancy's teaching me to use her computer." Nancy can't move her hands around the touch pad, so whispers to Joan how to start her movies and surf the web. When Joan returns the next morning, Nancy is gone.

Hospice literature teaches the patient will often give subtle signals of their awareness of when they will die. Nancy could not live on frozen slushed cookies alone. Unable to drink her usual espresso, I'd discovered that if I made one, then let it cool to body temperature, she could manage It. I trimmed a straw to a miniature espresso size, and devised a method to tape it to her cup. If I held her head in one hand and the cup in the other, she could drink a few sips through the straw. I occasionally gave her the count of our remaining pods, the sealed individual servings for her coffee maker. I told her— order more. One afternoon returning from a shopping outing, I asked her, "Did you order more? Only two weeks' supply left." She whispered—yes, she ordered plenty. They never came, and as she was so weak, it wasn't high enough on the priority list to ask. On the eleventh we still had a few pods left. I checked her Nespresso account. She had never ordered any refills.

I was not with Nancy when she died, one of many reasons for me to feel deep guilt and remorse for so many things I did wrong or didn't do at all. Early Friday morning she was sleeping and wheezing occasionally from hay fever. After checking on her one more time, I went upstairs to wash up, listening to her breathing on the baby monitor. The wheezing quieted and I relaxed, figuring her breathing was clearing and she could sleep more comfortably. Then I started to worry and I decided to check on her. In the dark at 5:30 a.m., I found her just as I left her, but not breathing. Unresponsive. I shook her, I called to her, and then I realized what had happened. I called hospice, and I called my brother. They confirmed what I thought I was seeing. I could do nothing but wait.

I paced the house. It was too early to call anyone else.

I had Nancy's Sirius radio set up to turn on Howard Stern every morning at 6:00 a.m., when his show started. I would ask her, "Do you really want Howard? Or maybe I should put on classical." Lately, she couldn't really answer, so I'd say "Classical?" and she'd nod no. Then I'd say "Howard?" and she would nod yes. Rita, our wonderful night on-call nurse, arrived just before six. She confirmed Nancy had died, and then Rita turned her attention to me. Was I in shock? I guess I was. We set to cleaning Nancy and preparing her to be picked up. I listened to the radio—it was Howard. How could Nancy die just thirty minutes before Howard came on? Wouldn't she hold on for that precious first hour? Then I remembered what she had told me last Friday when she opted for classical instead. Howard is in reruns on Fridays.

Because of her disease and drugs, Nancy experienced many vivid and sometimes disturbing dreams. She would wake wet with sweat at all hours and tell me, still somewhat under, what had terrified her in her sleep. In almost every dream, I had left her for extended travel to Asia or Europe, or I was on a bike ride, and she couldn't reach me. I began to realize how she had encouraged me to pursue all my crazy interests, all the while left with anxiety at being left alone. During the ten months she was confined to bed at home, when I was caring for her and we spent so many hours and days together, I came to realize how generous she had been, and how selfish I had been. And how unjust it was that it was she who lay dying.

But a couple of weeks ago, she released me from my debt of guilt. It was after three a.m., and neither of us had really slept yet. All her demons were out that night—physical and psychological, and every time the light went off, a new crisis came on and we awoke again. Maybe she hadn't slept at all, and I did whatever needed doing, from listening and wiping her down with cold towels, to a full bed and clothes change. As I cleaned her from the latest crisis, using her favorite foam and body wash, she kept apologizing, and I said what I always said,

"This is a 24/7 service, maid, nurse, and kitchen."

"No problem."

"I'm glad to do it."

I meant it. Who wouldn't? I'm strong like a bull; she's dying. Not facing me as I cleaned her back she said all I needed to hear, "When this is all over, you deserve the most expensive bike you can find and then go ride it anyplace."

She knew I wouldn't, but I knew she had signaled me that our accounts are in balance. From then on, we were equal partners to the end.

Death draws people to their faith and to God, they say. You know, I found the opposite. I didn't feel closer to any angels in heaven. I saw plenty of angels, all right here in Reston. Joan, our seventy-two-year-old nurse, who freelances doing daily care only for terminal cancer patients, made every one of Nancy's last days a joy. She worked overnight in a nursing home, stopped at her house for a shower and to prepare breakfast for her family, sometimes stopping to visit her mother at a nursing home, then arrived for a half-day of caring for Nancy—washing her, changing sheets, caring for her wounds, spooning ice, running her Mac, even cutting her flowers to keep the room pretty and fresh. Nancy's case nurse, Colleen, came every other day, sat with Nancy, and held her hand while they exchanged whispers. Colleen kissed Nancy every day coming and going, and when things were tough, gave me a hug and helped me to hang in there. My friend, Alan, brought Nancy the world's most expensive bedding and body wash, and he, too, held her hand and kissed the papery skin of her hollow cheeks.

The morning Nancy died, Alan and I had a ride scheduled. In my panic with nobody to talk to, I texted him, "No ride today—talk later. " Hours later, as the funeral home station wagon backed out our driveway with Nancy's washed and covered body inside on a stretcher, Alan walked in the door dressed to ride, with my fresh wheels he'd picked up for me at the race shop downtown and the first whole watermelon of the season. He looked at Nancy's bed— empty for the first time since her last trip to the hospital months ago, and then looked at me: "Ready to ride?" We rode a quick 50 miles, finishing at Adams-Greene funeral home in Herndon.

You know how many funeral homes there are? How to choose one? I knew Adams. I have passed it maybe fifteen times per week for the past fifteen years, and I always thought, "It's an old brick house, always been family owned, and with the most eclectic mix of clients, from the Fairfax County Mercedes/ Beemer families, to Sarah Palin's "real" Virginians tailgating with a keg in their parking lot. And like our house, our office, our hospital, and our grocery stores, it's right on the bike path. Alan and I walked in, a little damp from exertion, two high-end racing bikes, two pair of cycling shoes, two men in Lycra. No problem to Adams-Greene, but they did confirm we were the first cyclists to arrive still in helmets to make those final arrangements.

Our neighbor, Susan, works hard as a nurse, mother, and wife, but always had time to console me, to bring gifts for Nancy, and to sit with her so that I could get out for a swim or a ride. Nancy's friends from Manhattan, Ko and Diana, each got on trains and came to DC, then taxied to our house to see Nancy for just the few minutes she could handle before becoming too tired, and then they would start the long trek back. Valerie came to our house so often only to hear, "Nancy's asleep ,"or

"Nancy's too sick to see anyone." "No problem," Val would say, "I live close." Two days later, she 'd try again, and eventually she'd be at the door during a few clear minutes and cheer Nancy up.

Nancy's mom and sisters and my parents traveled to Virginia repeatedly just to sit in an empty hospital room and await Nancy's return from yet another procedure, or to sit in her room at home while she slept, secure knowing someone was nearby. My brother called every day to check on Nancy and came by every night he didn't have to be at a soccer match.

You know what's scary? Those New Age books people give you when you have cancer, the ones we science types laugh at, turn out to be completely right. It's not a question of "Are there angels?" There is an almost infinite number of angels, and they are all around us all the time. We just don't see them, even though they sometimes are living inside our own bodies.

April 17, 2008
To all of AeroAstro, a few at Radyne, and some friends who attended yesterday.

I don't see writing much email in the next day or three, but did not want twenty-four hours to go by without thanking all of you for helping me along in a difficult period not nearly over. Nor do I wish it to be. The journey is always important to me, and this is certainly one with the sort of proportions I tend to look for, albeit not a venue I would have chosen.

Cards, emails, flowers, visits, small gifts, making your own voyages to be with us yesterday, and at AeroAstro and Radyne, the flexibility to do what I've needed to do for Nancy, for our families, and for myself over the past several months has been overwhelming, and I think well beyond what I deserve. But I'll accept all this good will as gracefully as I can (with grace not being one of my fortes)—no arguments.

Seeing so many yesterday was a motivator for me to get things together and return to real life. I hadn't even thought about what we normally categorize as real life for quite a while. This experience is to me, sort of a personal Ramadan—a change of focus from the day-to-day. Yesterday, seeing all of you, helped me start to think about the rest of the flight plan—the part where the plane gradually descends and lands back on the ground. Hopefully, in accordance with the pilot's definition of a perfect landing, anyone with aircraft and inhabitants all remain in one piece.

See you all soon and thanks again for supporting and caring.

—Rick

April 18, 2008
(From a co-worker)

Three people I work with have lived through similar losses, and one of them summarized in the following email what they all said to me. I thought this was well said and a perspective earned from hard experience.

Returning to real life takes a long time and it is never the same once you begin to arrive.

Some cultures set aside a whole year for this process because the first year can be really rough, and we need a lot more time to grieve than many people understand. Most of the crowd will melt back to "normal" in a matter of weeks or months, seeing this as old news.

Yet some will remain, understanding that, for you, it will never be old news this year or next year or the one after that. These are the ones who have been to the shadowed valley and know the way through, and they are able and willing to help shepherd new arrivals past the darker times ahead. And the rest—we can be happy for them because they do not yet have a reason to understand.

—Ken

April 20, 2008
Lisa was an old friend of Nancy's—since biz school in the mid '80s. Lisa has a successful book in print and writes beautifully. I tracked her down via her book's web site, since I really didn't have any contact info for Nancy's LA friends. Luckily, that worked.

Lisa wrote:

Dear Rick,

It was indeed a shock to open your email just now and to discover that we have lost our beautiful, funny, kind, brave, whip-smart balletomane, and British-royalty aficionado, Nancy. I am so glad you were able to find me through the website. It never served a more important use.

I am filled with memories of all the wonderful times we all shared here in LA—the dinners, the cheesecakes, the music, the laughs. We were there when she met you all those years ago and your fateful date at the Hollywood

Bowl that seemed to go on for weeks and culminated in Nancy's announcement (to our utter amazement and not a little envy) that she knew you were THE guy, and that she was going to marry you. If she was anyone but Nancy, none of us would have given you guys more than a few months as husband and wife. But how we laughed, years later, as we met around yet another dinner table, to find you two still together and committed to one another—even through the strain of a commuter marriage when Nancy was working for American Ballet Theatre in New York.

The last time I saw her, we sat together in the empty theater and watched an ABT rehearsal at the Music Center. I remember my awe at her bravery in shouldering this huge job, contending with the outsized egos of the people she worked with, some of whom apparently were not very kind to her, and flying back and forth to Reston while being ill. This was a woman who lived much of her life on sheer will. And she did it so gracefully and, as you said, without complaint. I feel so lucky to have known her, and send you my deepest sympathy at a time I know must be unbearably hard.

For now, I will forward your email to both Joan who will know how to reach Nancy's USC and other friends, and to Ellyn. I'll also give some thought to who else I may know who knew Nancy. Walt also sends you his condolences. It will be good to see you again when you come out here in the fall.

All my love and support to you and to the family,
—Lisa

April 22, 2008

It's interesting to hear from others on two accounts (at least):

1) Their projection of what would make them feel better onto me. Not that I would expect anything different. It's fine, but it just says a lot about each person to hear what would, in essence, help them in this situation

2) Their recollections. Nancy was a complex person, and each person saw a different element of her, with little correlation sometimes. Multiple personalities—not as a pathology, but certainly there. But again, each person's perception is reflected in what they are like. A drama PhD friend of hers remembers her laugh and facial expressions. Another, who has just written a fictional novel based on her family's diaspora, sees Nancy in terms of her cooking and her relationships within and outside her family. A third sees her effectiveness in the arts world and her ability to multiplex work, marriage, dance, and cancer, etc.

You know, I see a religious similarity here. We know there is a lot to learn from this tragedy—a lot that can help us to understand our lives and the lives of others we care about. And yet, the lesson is obscure, hard to discern, ambiguous, and changes almost daily. Which makes me think of a criticism atheists make of religion and the Bible. They say, "Why doesn't almighty God just make Her point of view clear? Certainly, the Lord of All who created all could write better, not contradict Herself all over Her book, and in fact, create so many books, each claiming to be the only real deal."

But isn't that exactly like what's happened to me trying to make sense of and learn from this experience? Torah, Bible, the

Holy Scriptures, the Koran, and others, taken together are no less obscure, no less capable of deriving contrary lessons from their fables than real life. When I try to teach Lulu anything, I'm sure she feels just as confused. One day Rick's happy, the next day he's yelling at me, she must think. And I, her almighty, think—this cat just doesn't get it. Yet.

A year? If I'm better in a year, I'll be pleased. You know, one more philosophical thought: I ride a bike, and sometimes it rains. I still ride the bike, except I get wet, and sometimes hypothermic if I'm not prepared. I consider my life right now to be a bike ride through an enormous—let's say yearlong—rainstorm. I'd probably like the ride a lot better if it were warmer and sunnier, but even in the rain there are moments when you see things you can't see on a sunny day—waterfalls coming down hills along the road, cloud and light patterns, wet leaves, the road as a long strip of perfect mirror. I do see those things in my life right now. Is it worth it? No—a dry, sunny ride is "better." But in neither case is there really a choice. You just keep pedaling and hope for improvement. And be glad it's not getting any worse, since it always can.

—Rick

May 2, 2008
It was beautiful weather today—eighty degrees.

The weekly company lunch meeting went great. I'm amazed that I seem to be working exactly as always. In some ways maybe better, having picked up some needed perspective on things. In addition, people appreciate me more, knowing how it was without me.

It's also strange that I'm not lonely—I always liked being alone, as did Nancy. We had in common the lack of desire to have much human company, even each other often times.) It's still a major relief to be home without family, Nancy's friends, and nursing and medical staff and their equipment streaming in and out. The pressure of being on call 24/7 was getting to me too—I felt guilty even when I was in the shower.

Therefore, what I do suffer from, I think, is what one should suffer from—the loss of the soul mate and life partner. It's very tough. I also feel badly for all the others who were close to Nancy, and it turns out there were many. If I feel bad for myself, I know that's just the tip of that iceberg.

Most importantly, I haven't gotten over what happened to Nancy for her own sake. After all, I'm alive and can go out and be in the eighty-degree sunshine. I have years, decades, to get used to living without her and to go on pursuing things. Nancy has no more reality, and that is the thing I am most sorry about. I would have gladly gone in her place and left her with a few decades to enjoy life. She deserved them just as much as any of us, and in my own value system, more than many who live on to very old age.

The Kaddish really says it all, or looking at it as a scientist, I do believe that the universe is somehow sensible and intelligently ordered. So I'm not bitter or feel I've been somehow cheated or singled out. I realize this is the natural way of things, and I accept it. If anything, I feel more confident in being able to face reality than before all this. But that doesn't stop me from missing Nancy, even the fairly infirm version of Nancy I kept company with over the last few months. That's the issue that philosophy and religion and science can't address.

I am glad that at least I'm not distracted by all those more superficial issues, and the issue I am working on is the crux of this situation. In most things, the first step in making progress is figuring out what the problem is. And the fact that I can focus on that fundamental problem without being hassled by many practicalities is why things are going better than I thought they would. Being a swimmer and a cyclist, two very meditative hobbies (unlike, say, golf) and having all these various jobs at AeroAstro, Brown University, and writing, is helpful, too.

—Rick

May 11, 2008
Mom,

In the emotional rollercoaster department, things were bad again Saturday night and Sunday morning here, though I'm glad to be moved into the RI house and out of Virginia. I got a Yahrzeit candle, since today is the one-month anniversary, and I figured the appropriate way to manage would be to light the candle the night before. Nancy used to do this for her father every year at sunset on the night before his anniversary.

I admitted to Rabbi Steve that in fact I light a little candle every night, and I even composed my own little prayer. It's like you talking with your father—it makes me feel better. Nancy loved to light candles—for Shabbat, Chanukah—any occasion.

But things are in such disarray here in Rhode Island. I think I threw out all the matches since we couldn't store flammables, and I don't have a lighter, so I figured it's the thought that counts and just let the candle sit there unlit. In fact, that made it even more poignant.

I've unpacked everything, including Nancy's three pair of shoes she always wore here. You know, in this phase you still run across all these remembrances. It's funny, but as much as I do tend to be most emotional alone on the bike or in the pool, it also helps me to enough to feel good enough to go through the rest of the day. So after a couple hours of unpacking and throwing away and putting away, the sun was warm enough and I took off for four and a half hours on the bike. What a beautiful day today.

And with the good weather, the Del's trucks were out. You know Del's? Green-and-white trucks that sell a sort of frozen lemonade slush with bits of lemon in it. It's a Rhode Island institution. There used to be a Del's truck parked outside my dorm in the good weather way back in '72. Nancy never failed to get a small Del's if we passed one of their trucks. Then I passed Allie's Donuts—another RI institution. I used to bike with space for a donut in my seat bag and always on Sundays brought her one.

Therefore, while I'm indulging in my nostalgia for what isn't anymore, a song comes on my MP3 player with a tag line of that old Thomas Wolfe line: "You can never go home again." And it occurred to me—that's the essence of this experience. Home is a combination of people and places. One of my freshman year profs at Brown said that after being at college, home is not quite home anymore. He was preparing us for a psychological letdown at Thanksgiving, and he was right. You no longer live at your parents' house because you're now visiting the house, which was home your whole life, meaning it's not quite home anymore.

So life changes, and what was for a long time home is no longer home. I thought it was an interesting idea, and something everyone has experienced.

Problem is, a dorm is not home either, the family home is not home any more, and so students are just floating among a series of temporary homes. That's the student's lifestyle—as Lisa (my niece) is doing—flitting from place to place, always visiting, never staying. For us older people, we do have permanent homes—I have two of them! They are still home but they don't feel like home, because something has obviously changed.

My final thought du jour is that it's terribly disrespectful to waste life wallowing in how we wish things would have been. Here I was, riding my beloved Bianchi bike on a beautiful route along the Atlantic on a perfect spring day in my beloved RI. My body is (for a change) rested and uninjured, and I have no heavy-duty homework or deadlines tonight—just a bunch of work phone calls. Obviously were I in charge, I could have designed a better situation. However, I'm not in charge of anything other than my own reaction to what I can't change, and to do what I can about the things I might be able to create or change. I've really applied myself to the latter and luckily have the house in RI to show for all that effort—a project Nancy also applied herself to.

Which leads to my final cliché du jour, which is, what would Nancy have wanted? Clearly, that at least one of us would enjoy the results of all of our dreaming and scheming. Would she have wanted me to not enjoy it and to spend every day lamenting we didn't survive as a couple? Her big concern at the end was that her death would be a burden to me. Colleen, her visiting nurse, used to tell Nancy that she had done a good job preparing and providing for me by cleaning up the business matters, and that

I was a highly capable person, and she shouldn't worry. Colleen told her I would miss her, but I would go on just as she would have hoped. They had that conversation several times, and it was a real heartbreaker. Almost as bad as the "am I getting better" questions that came a few months earlier.

The house looks pretty decent. Everything is either in a box, or thrown away, and the clutter is zero or close to it. A lot of junk is not set up yet—e.g., no pictures hung, but at least it's clean, neat, and livable, and what's left are the nice-to-haves.

Tonight the temperature is dropping from the sixties to forty, windy already, and rain forecast to start overnight. Which rather underlines my philosophy that it's wrong to waste the sunny days we have. They are rare enough as it is.

—Rick

May 25, 2008
Hi Steve,

Adding to my collection of thoughts.

I could go on and on, and I mention in my satellite textbook that for some reason our society sectors off technical things into a box labeled "Irrelevant to Daily Life." Hence, we don't have street names, executive desk decorations, or town monuments to technical devices, principles, etc. In Göttingen, Germany, a university town where I did an internship, they had a little of that since Carl Friedrich Gauss and other heavies did their work there.

Looking at the history of mathematics, the Greeks particularly built philosophies around numbers. They got started probably from the Babylonians. They really liked the integers. Each one had colors and moods associated with it. These became integrated, for instance, into Cabalist thought also. I'm sure you know these appear in the Old Testament as well. Hebrew prefers pairs. Japanese avoid groups of four.

In the Aristotelian world, rationality was important, and that extended to rational numbers—numbers that can be represented by either a finite number of digits (2.5, the ratio of 5 over 2) or repeating sequences (1/3 = 0.33333 ...). They did *not* like irrationals—square root of 2, pi. They, for a long time, denied these numbers even existed, claiming that they were in fact rational, but we just hadn't figured them out yet, or that they were not really numbers!

In fact, in infinity theory, there are infinitely more irrational numbers than rational numbers. That is, between any two rational numbers, there is infinity of irrational numbers. Rationals (including integers) are the oddity—irrationals are the majority—infinitely more common. Of course, twenty-first century humans have gotten over all that. Not exactly. We believe that all diseases have cures and all problems have solutions. Just maybe we haven't found them yet—the same thinking the Greek rationalists applied to pi.

Let's face it, I say. There are actually very few answers, and useful as they are (the number 2.5 is pretty useful, not to mention 1, 2, 3, and 12, to name a few of my favorite integers), I believe there are infinitely more questions that can't be answered than can be. Yet when we identify one of them—my personal fixation at this moment being death—we paper it over with literature, liturgy, faiths, and philosophies, all attempting in their own way, to rationalize it.

Okay, I've only grappled with death in an intense way for less than a year, but my tentative conclusion is it is the pi of human experience. We can approximate it; we can even talk about it and use it. But we can never, despite its common occurrence in everyday life, fully describe, explain or "solve" it. (And what is more common than a circle, whose simple ratio of circumference to diameter is pi? So pi is as common as sunlight.)

After a couple thousand years grappling with irrationals, we have learned to appreciate their beauty and their mystery. They are not outlawed numbers. We now call them "natural" numbers, since they so dominate the natural world and any numbering system. Maybe two thousand years from now (maybe fewer?), people will accept certain common features of human experience as "natural" and appreciate their mystery and their lack of a solution.

This is not to say there's no role for religion, literature, philosophy, etc. There is a lot of utility in knowing pi to 3, 10, even 20 digits. There's no use to bother expressing it out to 20,000 digits, since nothing humans do is that precise. It's just a string of random numbers (in fact, calculating pi's digits is a good way to generate a purely random sequence). There may be similarly no use to rationalizing death to too many "digits."

—Rick

May 29, 2008
My diary page for today.

I'm ok during the day. Sleep is the hard part. I can't control what I dream about, and it's always disturbing. I imagine as the poignancy fades, so will that problem. I'm giving myself six months (four and a quarter to go) to see if I'm getting over that problem. During the day I'm keeping it together, and the way my mother-in-law and Nancy (used to) dance, I use the pool and bike. Those are my contemplative times, plus when I write. I'm now reading yet another book on grief. This one is excellent. I can send you details if you care.

Some things in life are like a bike ride—an hour, a day, a week, a month, and they end. But other things signal a permanent change. Dense as I am on these things, I'm realizing that the acute phase probably is finite, but the lasting loss is permanent. This is the beginning of a new phase of life, and I need to realize that this is not a detour, but a completely new route to a new destination. As Karen, Nancy's older sister from Rutgers said today when we spoke, "It's hard to get arms around that."

I will say I feel Nancy living inside me in some respects. When things happen to me, sometimes I feel like two people are perceiving a situation at the same time—my old way of looking at things "my way" in parallel with Nancy's perspective. I find it almost therapeutic to act "on her behalf" when I'm in a situation she was better at than I am, e.g., office politics and the management of free time and family. She was my senior advisor on all those things. Granted, there's nothing like the real thing, but I'm doing my best to emulate her expertise.

—Rick

June 2, 2008

To say I haven't believed in ritual is an understatement. I have resented imposition of doing rituals on me ever since prayer before meals at YMCA camp forty years ago. In addition, my rationalist, materialist scientific mind rejects them as nonsensical. When my swimming opponents crossed themselves on the block before the starting gun, did they believe God would grant them a victory over me because I didn't pray? How much did prayer serve the concentration camp victors and their families? Prayer is a conversation—one you're having with yourself.

Craven is a personal put-down word for me. When I see competitors blatantly suffering—unzipping jerseys down to their waists, grimacing, and losing the ability to smile or socialize under the weight of concentrating in order to block pain, I know they are not real athletes. They are acting out like a child with a temper. My strategy is to stay zipped, friendly, and cool, focusing my mental and physical energy on the task, not the display for the crowd I think I'll impress with the suffering I can endure. Acting out is a ritual—no crowd ever pushed a racer over the line.

Considering myself a ritual rejecter, I didn't even realize all the rituals I have practiced to help myself live with Nancy's loss and mine. Some of them are common, ancient practices, but most I invented without realizing they were rituals. I was just doing what I felt I needed to do.

AeroAstro launched our first satellite in 1992, and for a number of reasons it had serious, life threatening problems. Unknown to us, it had been dangerously modified before launch, and the launch itself was more stressful than planned. After the first few passes over our ground station at Los Alamos, New Mexico, most of the team involved with the spacecraft, including the customer, believed it was lost. Some of us, myself included, had experienced saving presumably lost spacecraft before, and we held out hope. We launched ourselves into an all-out effort to save ALEXIS, as she was known, an acronym that matched the name of a then-popular TV heroine.

During two months of round-the-clock, mostly ineffective efforts, one of our team, Bob, began a ritual of his own. He assembled a small shrine to the satellite—arranging its mission logo patch, engineering drawings, and a small 3-D solid model in a corner of his cubicle. Every day when he arrived at the office, he lit a single white candle, said a small prayer, and set to his tasks by the light of that candle. Ten weeks after the ritual began, on the Fourth of July weekend, a skeleton crew was attempting the latest uplink of new commands. For the first time since the April launch, ALEXIS answered. We were soon in full operating mode and the spacecraft went on to a highly successful mission that lasted over ten times its original design specification.

What role did Bob's shrine and candles play? At the time I knew the answer—none at all. Now I realize that at the start of every demanding, and probably fruitless, day of difficult work, Bob was confirming his personal commitment to our mission. It motivated him to do his own miracles. And who among the rest of us could give up, seeing how deeply the satellite's crisis had touched and motivated Bob? People saved ALEXIS, but Bob's shrine helped those people work each of their miracles.

Nancy also enjoyed rituals, and, like her love of T-bone steak, I supported them though I didn't personally indulge in them. She loved the Shabbat candles and the Chanuka candles. She lit a Yahrzeit candle every anniversary of her father's premature death from bone marrow cancer. When we moved into a new house, she brought bread and salt. She never would give a gift of knives, and she practiced the Japanese aversion to giving a gift composed of four of anything. She had a special pair of pink Converse All-Stars she wore to every medical procedure and never on other occasions. After she left her job leading the finance operations of the Kennedy Center, she never again took their logo jacket she had worn for almost ten years out of the closet.

But it was the candles I most remembered, and I began the practice, every evening, of lighting a candle for Nancy. I didn't think of it as a ritual—I thought about doing what she would do in my situation and honoring her memory through her love of candlelight. When she lit the candles, she would hurriedly mumble her way through the appropriate Baruch at a pace akin to the legal disclaimers at the end of ads for automobile insurance. I modified her prayer to make her the focus and whispered it to myself. Two months later, I'm still practicing that act, which I now recognize as a ritual.

But another ritual preceded that one. For the last four months of her life, I slept on the floor next to her bed, without a mat and with a single pillow. It was uncomfortable, but I did it to experience a minute fraction of the discomfort she lived with, not just at night, but 24/7. And it was practical. My last words to her every night were, "I'm right here if you need anything." I could hear her breathing, and if she awoke, I awoke. Deep sleep on the hard floor wasn't possible and under the circumstances, neither was it desirable. I didn't want to substitute an electronic gadget for the physicality of being there, but what I called my Zen Bed was itself a ritual. The day she died, my brother suggested I might comfort myself by sleeping in a real bed. I hadn't even thought of it, but on consideration, I lay on that floor next to her empty hospita-style bed with my single small pillow and cried myself to sleep one last night in our final living arrangement. The next morning, I moved myself back to our regular bedroom, unused since December, telling myself I had to face it, its memories, and the transition back to a life not centered around care of Nancy.

In conversation with Rabbi Steve, I recalled how I had memorized equations in preparation for my PhD qualifying exams. I taped them to my bicycle's handlebars, and, during the long hours on the road, looked at them until after a while they stuck in my memory. Then I would write new equations and tape them down over the old ones. That memory gave me a new idea, and I printed out psalms Steve recommended and posted them on my refrigerator with fridge magnets. My ritual then was to read an entire psalm each time I would go to the refrigerator. I didn't allow myself to open the door until I read the entire psalm for the short ones, or a verse of a longer one.

Nancy used to contribute money to the Catholic Diocese of Washington in the memory of the father of her best friend who was a devout follower of the Church and had died a few years earlier of cancer. This earned her frequent mailings from the church. A few days after Nancy died, mail came from them— rosary beads with an instruction booklet on praying the rosary. Now for a little musical interlude.

Nancy and I shared a propensity for contrarianism. Mine is overt; I rejected ritual when my parents tried to instill it in me via attendance at temple. I waged my wars over not being religious and selfishly fought a successful campaign to not participate in a bar mitzvah. I started a small satellite company to overtly reject the dogma of the space establishment on how space engineering should be done. When I lived in New York, I never wore any black clothes, because black is the easy way to say, "I'm a native," on the street. Instead, I purposely dressed like a tourist in soft light tennis shoes and a big Australian tennis hat.

Nancy's challenge of the status quo was more subtle. When all her biz school classmates took high paying jobs at major US corporations, she accepted a low-paying accounting job at the LA Philharmonic. A native of LA, she moved to DC and used to say that LA people were all soft and couldn't handle rain, let alone our ice, snow, mosquitoes, and humidity. And though she lived and thought as a Jew, she often wore a crucifix on her necklace—usually a heavy, ornate gothic one. And how many cute young MBAs living in quiet suburbia blast Howard Stern every morning at 6:00 a.m., and go to work wearing, on one wrist, a yellow Lance Armstrong LIVESTRONG bracelet, and on the other, an ID bracelet from Tiffany, inscribed, simply "Howard"?

I took the blue rosary beads on their faux-silver necklace out of the envelope and hung them on the calendar in my bathroom, where I would see them every morning and evening. Nancy would have been happy to leave them somewhere around the house, advertising her nonslavery to her religion.

From her days as a cyclist, one of the first casualties of her disease, she had a remarkable collection of those short-top, brightly-colored cycling socks. I wear one of her pair over my own socks every time I ride.

Unpacking and moving back into our Rhode Island house, I found her trusty Merrill hiking shoes, warm hat ,and gloves. All way too small for me, they have a permanent place in my small closet.

Though a big fan of Howard Stern, Nancy never developed the calloused ear of lovers of very hard, acidic rock. That was my department, abiding with my love of more mainstream pop. Whenever I hear a song on my radio that reminds me of her—either in message or memory, hearing it during our times together, I record it. I have slowly collected a long mix of Nancy music.

Nancy had a particular Google home page featuring a friendly Japanese farmer fox who kept a watermelon patch, played Shamisen, and fished in his pond. I made that my home page in spite of my contrarian's disdain of Google's ubiquity.

Nancy and I used to swim together, and afterwards she would challenge me: How many laps? I would argue that as she wore the small fins called Zoomers, the comparison was unfair. But she'd have none of that. The competition raged for years. Now when I reach the end of my swim, I do one more down and back—just to irk her with my 82 vs. her 80.

What are all these crazy things if not rituals? I refuse to talk to Nancy because I don't want to deny death. On the contrary, I have to keep telling myself she's not coming back. And I can hedge. If I'm wrong, she already knows what I would say—I don't need to verbalize. So for whom am I practicing all these little rituals? Like Bob's shrine to our errant satellite, they fortify me, and they help me to go on. They are not symptoms of a belief in the irrational and unseen—they are the writing on the pavement of the great Tour de France climbs, urging the top riders to carry on despite cold, sometimes snow, danger, injury, pain, and fatigue.

—Rick

June 2, 2008
I guess I've had a lot on my mind ...

The Death of Death is a great title, but a lousy thesis. It feeds our deep-seated desire to believe that death is not the end, but more like a one-way airline ticket to an exotic destination so wondrous that nobody ever wants to return. Maybe that works for some people, and God bless them. Count me among the majority of Western people who fundamentally cannot believe in an afterlife. We are professional skeptics. Or so we tell ourselves.

But we happily drink the societal Kool-Aid of the good death and its twin manifestations.

I was relieved of the first myth within forty-eight hours of Nancy's death. I felt enormous guilt that I hadn't been with her when she died. I should have known something was different—she had not yet awoken more than thirty minutes after her habitual time, and her breathing sounded markedly different—slower, more rhythmic, and more verbalized, a sigh emanating with every exhale, almost resembling her nickname of me. But I didn't want to disturb her just because the clock read a particular time and went upstairs for my shower and shave. Fifteen minutes later, I returned to find her gone. She might have been terrified, too weak to call out to me—or maybe I missed her call submerged by the din of the shower? After months of 24/7 surveillance, how could I have missed holding her hand at the most critical moment of passage?

My friend Steve lost his wife a few years ago, and he witnessed her final seconds, along with their hospice nurse. When I related my anxiety, he told me that having been there—it's not like TV. She didn't open her eyes and look lovingly into his, squeeze his hand, say goodbye, smile, and pass peacefully into her good night. "Not exactly," Steve said, with an edge that told me I didn't want to know what he had experienced. My hospice nurse confirmed that many, maybe most, dying people don't want an audience, either preferring privacy, or to save others from standing too close to the flame.

Yet the New York Times obituaries always say "... died surrounded by loving family." Don't we all want to believe that fantasy of the if not happy, surely contented and loving death?

So much for the theatrics of the good death. As Nancy would say, "It ain't happening."

More dazzling and so ubiquitous as to go unquestioned is the idea of good deaths and bad deaths, a ranking dependent on circumstances. A solider who goes to Iraq knowing he might die comes home in a casket, and we consider that an honorable and proper death for which his family should feel pride and patriotism. A child killed playing on the front lawn by a reckless and drunk driver has suffered a bad death, and the survivors are expected to be seriously injured, maybe even disabled by grief, bearing its scars for life. When grandma lives to her nineties and dies, she had a full life and it's a good death. When a highly productive, creative, and generous professional dies in mid-career, for instance Jim Henson, creator of the Muppets, who died of pneumonia in his late thirties, that is a tragedy, whereas another young person, less well known to the general public, dies of that same disease, and his death is ranked as less tragic.

Who would die slowly of Parkinson's, Alzheimer's, or Lou Gehrig's disease if they could suffer a sudden and unexpected heart attack on the eighteenth tee?

The reality is that none of us want to die, nor do we want to lose loved ones ever. The death of a fifty-year-old is no more or less tragic than the death of a five, twenty-five or eighty-five-year-old. Each of us has our plans, our friends, and family, or lacking even that, our own thoughts and interests, for ourselves or from our loved ones who would like to see us restored. The death of Karen Ann Quinlan was probably unnoticed by her, but it was a tragedy to the many surrounding her. Our media latched on to that tragedy despite her own lack of consciousness to a world of any imaginable kind.

My substitute for the good death/bad death conundrum? Good grieving and bad grieving. Labeling a death good or bad, or somewhere on a continuum in between, interferes with the facility of grieving. If the death is a good one, what excuse do we have to be so devastated by it? "Wasn't your son a strong and proud soldier who resolutely put his life on the line for his country?"—is not a question that helps a person reconcile with their feelings of loss. And labeling the abduction and murder of a college student a "bad death" only tells the family that it shouldn't have happened, and that the world is therefore unjust, and in fact cruelly flawed. That is a valid way to see things, but it is not the only way to order our universe, and it does not help the survivors to attempt the voyage to peace with their loss.

So who benefits from the philosophy of death on a grading curve? I suppose it sells books and movies—mostly about the bad ones that can be exploited to well up emotions in the audience. But I doubt even Hollywood has the clout to permeate society with a good/bad death mythology. I believe it taps into a fundamental of human evolution—survival of the fittest. We know that all living things select out for the "best"— the healthiest, the most reproductive, the most adaptable to a changing environment, the best competitors for resources. We cannot overestimate our propensity to constantly grade and evaluate everything. Fundamentally, our mate selection is about reproductive success, and our lives are, according to one extreme but ingenious philosophy, a mechanism by which we live out the aspirations of our DNA, which uses us to compete against other helical strands of carbon, nitrogen, and hydrogen.

Civilization depends on moderating base instincts. We are taught not to steal, not to murder, not to have incestuous relationships. We learn to postpone immediate gratification for future rewards. In fact, we even learn not to discriminate against people we consider lower on the natural selection ladder. Hence, we don't condone ethnic cleansing, both because it violates the truth that all ethnic differences are minor and in general, balanced, and because it violates our civilized commitment to protect those weaker and less fortunate. We fear violence and disorder because we don't want to live the *Lord of the Flies*.

Looking around, we grade and classify everything—*Consumer Reports* ranks automobiles, even though it's well known that if we were rational consumers, we'd make completely different choices. Diamonds are graded meticulously, even though some people might prefer a bigger diamond with some interesting carbon particles scattered inside it—I do, since I like the coexistence of the two phases of carbon. I think of a perfect diamond about as pretty as Millbrook bread—too uniform and unnatural. I like a few wheat grains in my bread and carbon in my diamond. We rank ourselves from that first measurement of length seconds after birth, through all the pre-college admissions tests, grade point averages, varsity letters accumulated, job offers, graduate school, personal bank balances, and the beauty of our spouses and homes. It never ends. Until death wipes it all clean again, but the process is already restarted in newborns. And even a funeral can be evaluated based on how real the tears are, how many cars are in the procession, whether a particularly highly ranked political leader shows up. Our measurements are so numerous, we can't measure them.

In measuring everything from figure skating to amateur singers, even to the point of achieving what we think is a meaningful ranking of an operatic performer vs. a rock star, or a chef's meal seen on TV, which we can't actually taste, we have failed to realize that this instinctive propensity to measure and to rank, like our propensity for reproduction, is necessary. It also needs to be moderated lest it rule, and ultimately ruin, the quality of our lives.

Having failed to see ranking as an instinct, which is destructive in excess, is it any surprise we cannot resist measuring death and ranking deaths like minivans on their attributes and debits? But just because the Chrysler Town & Country may be ranked not as good a value as its lower-priced, but fundamentally identical Dodge counterpart, plenty of well-informed consumers prefer the Town and Country van. Maybe they like the color, or maybe their mom chauffeured them from school to soccer practice or to Dairy Queen in one. It brings back memories of a more innocent time, before they realized that every aspect and moment of their existence would be subject to a societal metric to the highest rank of which they are compelled both to aspire and ultimately to fall well short of the top.

It is a shame that we have only ten fingers and hence a base ten numbering system. If we had one more, perhaps there would have been room for an eleventh commandment— "Thou shalt not indulge in ranking, for all God's creations are miraculous. "including, good or bad, death.

—Rick

June 2, 2008

After all my updates on Nancy concluded April 11, a friend remarked that the email silence since has left a void in her inbox. Though that's a feeling I think most of us can only aspire to, I'm taking her suggestion to send you this follow-up email, roughly two months after Nancy's death.

My writer's block is that I have avoided this experience being about me. Many people who grieve are not really grieving for the person who died, or not entirely. They have to face loneliness, which they don't like, or handling household things the other person used to do for them, or financial insecurity. None of those are an issue for me. Luckily, I already have a job; I always took care of the "physical plant" except financing, which is now being handled by my "personal CFO" (aka accountant); and I don't tend to need much company. A dichotomy of our relationship as a couple was our shared enjoyment of solitude and mutual respect for each other's privacy and freedom of action. And after months of our house being converted to a sort of clinic cum hotel, with my own personal schedule filled with the rhythms of hospice care, I welcome the silence and lack of structure not as lonely, but as a refreshing opportunity to be with and look after myself.

What I mourn is what I think we all feel—the loss of sharing life with a person we loved. That version of our lives is no longer available to us. And most of all, I feel empathy for what Nancy endured. Selfish though it may be, who can watch her experience at close range and not hope somewhere in the ego that we never are faced with what she faced? But our id knows, just as grief's an inevitable side effect of love, death is the companion of life. Neither can exist without the other. Music, my high school orchestra conductor, used to say to get us to quiet down, is a painting on a canvas of silence.

I sometimes see humanity as a giant ant colony. We are all busily doing our minuscule part of building the whole. And when an event destroys some of us and some of what we have built, we who survive are immediately and energetically all over that scar, examining, clearing, and rebuilding. I used to think of ants as idiots. Don't they realize one clumsy footprint could have squished them and not the others? What in the world motivates them to expend all that energy, given the next insult may be one footstep away? Now I realize what they have known eternally and I didn't. So what? Life is the business of building, losing, and rebuilding. We all go on, at least subconsciously, even if we don't believe we can. And despite what Ayn Rand says, when we die, the rest of our colony copes and progresses.

As I had immersed myself in the literature on cancer, home care, hospice, and death and dying, I'm now reading intensively about grief. If you one day find yourself, or a friend or loved one, in my situation (come to think of it, today might be such a day), I recommend the book, *On Grief and Grieving*, by the late Elisabeth Kübler-Ross and David Kessler. It anticipates and thinks through my recent feelings and experiences much more clearly than I would like to admit. As John Lennon said, more or less, "There is nothing we can do that hasn't been done, nothing we can feel that hasn't been felt," death, loss, and learning a new way of life in their slipstream are a shared human experience.

I have benefited from a lot of help from my family, from Rabbi Steve, from many friends and readers of these essays, from hospice, from the solitude of cycling the open road, swimming, running on the beach and through woods and cities, and from the reading what people have recommended to me. Hardest is to shift the focus. It is so easy and fulfilling dedicating one's life to a person we love who is in need. And when they are gone, when all the trials and struggles and disappointments, the coming to terms with the reality—when it is over, life feels like a fire in a desolate clearing or maybe in a dark forest in Siberia. Heat and light are all around—the crackling and seething sounds, the sweet acrid smells of a beautiful, warming fire, but it lacks benefit. We're not even able to witness and be cognizant of it. Steven Gould wrote that physics figures out the plumbing of the universe, how it works, and what holds it all together. But only religion and the spirit address the why. I know every day the mechanism is working, but where is the ghost who used to live in my machine, whose soul shined out through its headlights? Chemical thermodynamicists can tell you all about fire; however, there's no equation or state diagram to describe its feeling and meaning to those who sit by it, nor the dismay we feel about a fire with no one nearby to benefit from its warmth.

Some of the advice I got was to get off my ass and get back to work. I think it's Nancy who most often gave me that advice, almost since we first met and regularly ever after. She was the hard worker and I am forever a slacker. I've taken her advice and resumed my full load at AeroAstro and at Brown. I moved back into the house in Rhode Island we rebuilt last winter and returned to my itinerant lifestyle, commuting among cities, doing long bike rides and other irrational athletic pursuits, and planning travel and possibly even some opportunities for temporary work assignments abroad. I put some faith in behaviorism—if you can act healthy, you can become healthy. Or as my brother put it conversely, "You can only get so well confined within an eleven-by-thirteen-foot hospital room."

I have learned a few things from twenty-five-plus years with Nancy, and her insights are now more available to me than when she was alive. Because I can no longer rely on her for them, the part of me that learned her has now come alive. In personal decisions, in managing at work, as every little decision and event comes up in the details of everyday life, I have a sense of her take and of my own. I find myself holding up both sides of the discussion. And that is the advice I would give to others.

They say in the Hallmark cards that the pleasant memories of the person and the times we had together will be a comfort to me. They are not. They make me cry, and I don't look forward to sleeping because I know she will appear in my dreams and I'll have to awaken to reality. I hope and believe that I can one day look back at things through that nostalgic sheen.

However, what does strengthen and comfort me are her thoughts, her preferences, her ways of doing, and her brand of initiative that live on, albeit at lower fidelity, within me. I have always considered myself a naïve and inappropriately happy child of a Midwestern upbringing, lacking the cool cynicism of my more sophisticated acquaintances who grew up in the great urban centers of the East and West coasts. Nancy, by contrast, had no patience for platitudes like looking on the sunny side of life or anything else. She taught me, more than any one thing, that life is worth living, even seen for what it is—in its full form—beauty, cruelty, love, and pointlessness—all of it. Her realism, compared with my unrelenting optimism, allowed her to appreciate her life even as so many parts of it were taken from her. Her expectations never over- nor undershot the realities available to her. She combined the ability to be turned on by life with an inability to be disillusioned by it.

So, back to that advice. How to do something for a person who no longer exists? That is the cosmic question I think we all face. I keep her alive, not through remembering times spent together, as that is too hard, but by turning over a part of who I am and how I think and perceive to her mental software. Some part of her does live inside me, and I'm doing my best to give it a comfortable accommodation and an outlet into this world she no longer exists within. I have augmented, or at least put a symbol upon, that little project with a few rituals. I know my rituals are, compared with life and death, nothing but triviality. But in that context, what isn't? I admit to wearing selections from her comprehensive collection of cycling socks, accumulated in healthier times, every time I go out on the bike. I swim an extra down and back for her every time I do a swim practice. I talk to Lulu the way Nancy talked to Lulu. I drive around in her yellow Beetle, complete with the yellow and pink roses in its vase. I get enjoyment and some small comfort in these funny little things as being her reach back into this world.

Of course there are limits. I'm not eating steaks at Morton's. Nancy brought balance to my life, and now I have to walk the beam without my coach's hand on my hip. I think for each of you who patiently followed my emails for the past year, she brought something to your life. This is your moment. Your certified flight instructor has stepped out of the plane after the harsh landing of April 11, and it's your time to solo. Students never think they are ready—none of them. Never. But all of mine managed to get the plane off the ground and back down, airframe and pilot in one piece. So can we.

—Rick

July 25, 2008

Fridays, today being the fifteenth Friday anniversary, have become my anniversary of loss. I give Nancy every early morning between 4:30 and 5:30, but on Friday mornings I light my candle. Fridays I say my prayer out loud, and I apologize for not being with her at the very end.

Do I have regrets? Definitely. Regret is a part of life's landscape, just as rain is a part of bike-riding's landscape. If you don't ride in the rain, you don't fully appreciate cycling. Rain isn't really avoidable, and neither is regret. Nancy used to say, "Bicycling is an outdoor sport." So is living. We all have regrets. I have many—actions I wish I had done, things I wish I had the courage to say, and many more that I wish I hadn't done or said. As you say, Nancy is still teaching me.

I don't regret my regrets any more than my rain rides. They make me feel more of a 360° person, a complete person. I appreciate life more, I live more carefully, I sense each moment rather than living always in the future. I am not a sociable person, but I enjoy human interactions much more. I realize how lucky I am to be able to play in that arena, to be a part of societal life—an ability lost to the sick and dying, who sense that loss acutely. How can I dismiss its attractions completely? With students and faculty, employees and colleagues, with athletes and even with the bureaucrats at the Rhode Island Department of Motor Vehicles, I appreciate my ability to interact with others, especially at their locations in offices, classrooms, or on the road. When I ride, I look at my shadow—the ability to cast a shadow is temporal—you have to be alive and exist; you have to be outdoors; the sun has to be shining. A shadow is a combination of rare opportunities realized.

My number one regret is not that I wasn't with her at 5:00 a.m. on April 11. It is that I didn't understand her anger, especially when I would be away—on the bike or even buying supplies for her. Through reading and thinking, I understand anger is a manifestation of fear. What were those fears? Fear of death? I don't think so. We're all going to die, except maybe Woody Allen. We don't fear it all day every day. A more frequent fear, more incessant, is the fear we won't be loved. And for a person sick limited to a bed and totally dependent on the goodwill of others, the fear is of no longer being loved, but merely being tolerated and serviced out of guilt rather than love. That's real and it's constant. Our pets share that fear. They don't need to be fed so much as to sense they are being fed out of love, not obligation to not be responsible for their starvation. Hunger for love is stronger than for food. A cat can find food in the grass and on the deck—but love is more elusive. When the tasks of love turn to tasks of routine and obligation, those fears manifest as anger even in a dog or a cat.

Nancy feared I wouldn't love her anymore, now that she was sick, unable to participate in activities, and required sometimes unpleasant physical care 'round the clock. If I didn't love her, she might be abandoned, psychologically if not physically, and in that sense die alone and a failure at sharing love with another person. Inability to be loved, the loss of a love, is our deepest fear and source of our anger. Not death, which is inevitable for all of us and thus not a failure. Loss of love is true failure. Loss of love is the root of fear, and that fear manifests in anger. I regret I responded to her anger, addressing that as the problem, rather than quelling its fundamentals.

What I do with that regret is what matters now. I was not then, nor will I ever be, able to understand everything, especially in its moment. Very few writers are real-time people. When you see a writer who is adroit with banter in a crowd, capable in real time, you wonder—is he genuine? Now that the real-time crisis is history, there is time to learn I can be grateful that Nancy is still teaching me.

—Rick

July 30, 2008
Passages (Part of a presentation to AeroAstro employes at a company-wide meeting)

This has been a year of changes, and by Friday, August 1, there will be another transition: on the first anniversary of Radyne's purchase of AeroAstro, Comtech's purchase of Radyne will be completed. Our name will officially change to Comtech AeroAstro Inc. Paul and I have agreed that with this transition, he will take over the role and title of president, and I will be focusing on special projects within the company on roughly a half-time basis.

In the seventies when popular psychology was, well, popular, the book, *Passages*, was a best seller, though its theme, that in every decade of life people reorient their goals and lifestyle preferences was just a little too tidy. Its more basic message has proven true for most people, and for companies, countries, and even earth's geology and climate. Change is not a continuous process. Rather, we each experience long periods of equilibrium punctuated by triggering events that initiate brief episodes of change, leading to a new period of equilibrium. College graduation is an example of an event that triggers change. Leaving college can begin a sequence of changes in employment, housing, family relationships, living location, even wardrobe and hair style—and then a new quiescent period of enjoying your new status as a working person. Until the next passage—maybe marriage, a first child, or a phone call from a friend across the country who is starting a new company.

AeroAstro was the focus of my professional life for over twenty years. I wrote its first business plan in 1987, though it took over a year to figure out what the company's initial strategy would be and to start operations. Twenty-plus years is a long equilibrium for anyone, especially me. In the past year, several big events occurred—our purchase by Radyne, the culmination of Nancy's and my long struggle with cancer, publication of my first nontechnical book, and now the purchase of Radyne by Comtech. Part of my motivation to take my long-postponed sabbatical was to work down my backlog of papers, courses, and other projects. It also provided an opportunity to plan my own passage, my accommodation to these big events.

Mark Ludwig's model—that companies grow logarithmically and in half-decade steps—i.e., very approximately $1 million, then $3 million, then $10 million, etc., and achieve equilibrium at each of those sizes—is another example of the *Passages* model. AeroAstro has experienced the $300,000 level, the $1 million level, the $3 million level, and the $10 million level. We are now in a period of striving to break through to the $30 million plateau. Each of these sizes is an equilibrium for many reasons. Each requires a different corporate organizational structure, a different style of management, a different way of doing sales, engineering, marketing, financial accounting, and changes in product mix. Optimized around being a $10 million company, a lot has to evolve to stabilize at the $30 million level. We are seeing big and small changes all around us—in physical plant, in adjustments to the org chart, in new ways of doing time cards, program management—along with new tools like MPM, Solomon, and others.

These changes are all moves into new territory. They are not always smooth and likely include some discomfort. But as a company, we are more dynamic, more important in our markets, and a more interesting place to work because in part we do choose to grow and to undertake the changes necessary to affect the passage to each new level.

AeroAstro's upper management team is an outstanding group of people, each highly capable and focused on the success of the company. Now being led by Paul with new energy, ideas, and initiatives, the team is a key element in our graduation to a new, larger company size. I can't say '08 or '09 or '10 is our year to reach the next equilibrium, but the pieces are coming together, and I believe it will happen—probably nonlinearly and in some unexpected ways.

My role at AeroAstro, which I have worked out collaboratively with Paul and with Radyne and Comtech, is to focus my professional efforts in a few different areas: AeroAstro, teaching and consulting, and writing. My focus at AeroAstro is on innovation across several business areas including marketing and corporate positioning, new products, new customers, and new relationships, including for example, an AeroAstro/university degree program. I think there's general agreement that these innovation areas are both important elements contributing to continued growth and a part of the set of new initiatives, which I am positioned, inclined, and qualified to make happen.

The amount of time I spend at AeroAstro will vary depending on the company's needs and how many projects I'm pursuing—but roughly halftime. I will operate mainly remotely from Rhode Island, but like other remotes, and maybe more than many, I'll be at Ashburn and in the Colorado office on a regular basis. Though my role has changed, my commitment to doing what is best for AeroAstro has not. I believe this new role for me, and Paul's promotion to president, is our best positioning to support AeroAstro's continued success. I welcome your suggestions on initiatives I might tackle and encourage your support of Paul and the upper managers. I'm working to create a stronger, larger, and more capable company with enhanced importance and influence in shaping the future of space and communications.

Thanks!

—Rick

Maccabees

Courtesy David Ascalon of Ascalon Studios

August 8, 2008

Here's one of my daily thoughts on survivor guilt—my current mental exercise.

I had to cycle into DC Thursday and had a couple hours on the bike to reflect on everything. Thursday evenings are my sort of Nancy remembrance weekly kickoff.

I think I have a mild case of multiple survivor guilt. Nancy and I really did work in partnership on her disease, and on many other things, which is no different from many married couples. Illogical though it may seem, one comes to feel your fates are entwined; not consciously, it's just a natural thing. You are both working on a common problem, so for one to survive and the other not—I never entertained that possible outcome. Yet it's a completely different situation to be on my side of the event than hers. I'm alive and well with maybe fifty years in front of me. She's not, to state the obvious.

Then I look at the purchase of AeroAstro by Radyne last year that Nancy largely facilitated. I mean, I built the company, but she got all the business details in place that allowed it to work. Again, an asymmetrical team effort. Top management of Radyne all came into it as we did—it was an honest attempt to build a better business, no smoke and mirrors on either side. Again, we all worked together, more or less, and one again comes to think, "We're in this together." But now I have my job and the luxury to tailor it to my liking, plus I am making money on my share holdings. While all of the Radyne execs have much more prestigious and higher paid jobs than mine, none own enough equity to realize a financial gain on sale. And many others in Radyne, including the entire board, which was made up of much more senior and accomplished people than I am, were simply discarded by Comtech. They are all—every one of them, and we're talking maybe fifteen professionals—job hunting, and I'm trying to help them. How did that happen?

So, in some sense, I survived twice, and both times through no particular genius or action on my own part. That's just the way the external forces played out. In the Radyne/Comtech case, it wasn't not life or death, but there's an analogy with being in any disaster and coming out not just alive, but in fact much better off, for which I'm very grateful. For my selfish self, this year has been one of great accomplishment, normally one for a real celebration—while almost all the others who worked on these things with me they either died or suffered loss of their job and often loss of potential financial benefits in the future.

There's nothing to be done? One does what one can for the living—that's why I'm spending a couple of days in San Francisco helping Radyne's CEO, who used to be my boss, find a job. For Nancy, the tragedy is much greater, and what can be done? Much less. People are basically about action, and in her case there is no action. So the alternative is thinking, talking, philosophizing, donating clothes to charity, thinking, "What would she do or like me to do?", lighting candles, saying my little prayers, writing her book, and other quasi-rational coping mechanisms, which sort of tell us, we're helping the deceased, but bottom line, on anniversary week number seventeen, there is no helping them. We're left to help ourselves, which is much less, if at all, satisfying.

Finally, two lessons from cycling. One is Steve is right. It's a ritual, and the never-changing look of the road—the asphalt and its myriad personalities—is a familiar face I've stared at over the handlebars since way before Nancy. It's like seeing the face of an old friend.

Cycling is not always a pleasure. The role of the cyclist is to find a way to enjoy even those tough times when the wind is head-on, sun is a killer, or the rain is soaking you (I got both yesterday via a thunderstorm in Maryland), legs are sore, the body wants to lie flat on the ground and give up, and your mind is wondering—what the hell am I doing out here? And the attractive aspect of those moments is?

Cyclists say the cure for everything is keep turning the pedals. And in a few minutes, or an hour or two, things eventually improve, you get your groove back, and you enter a period so good it seems worth the bad times. Isn't that what we all experience in jobs, in family, in grieving and loss, and possibly even in survival, which is ultimately life's greatest challenge and satisfaction? I see it in the eyes and in the muscular bodies under mottled grey coats of the deer who live by my Rhode Island house in the winter. They take great pride in their ability to live through the New England winter, family intact, wandering among the sand bars, shoreline crusted with frost, searching freeze-dried berries off the bushes, under a grey sky, across the January salt pond frozen solid. The deer, cyclists, the families who survive loss, we keep on whatever, and we all deserve some pride just in doing life's daily work as long as we have that opportunity.

—Rick

This professional photograph is apparently from Madison Square Park, 23rd and Broadway, which Nancy and I would pass as I walked her to work every morning at American Ballet Theatre. We would see homeless men sitting, each of those days, on the wood and wrought iron benches facing Broadway. Was this his day of regret for what his life might have been? Or maybe he enjoys his life. Many homeless do, but regret some other loss—of a friend, maybe. Regret is all we really know about this man on that day, his partaking of that ingredient of the human experience.

August 8, 2008—Three-Month Anniversary
Maybe via my emails you're thinking I've abandoned a life of science and rationality, maybe even traded my calculator and *CRC Handbook of Chemistry and Physics* in for a Ouija board and deck of tarot cards. I've reexamined a lot in the past year, and on balance my beliefs in the value of material science and of the spirit in living have emerged if anything stronger.

If I have lost faith, it is in illusions of immortality and control. I have questioned if humans ever gained the clearer vision of the universe we have sought throughout history—in mathematics, science, philosophy, and religion. Could we handle that truth? That it takes thousands of years to even marginally widen our sights may be fortuitous—like at sunrise, when nature gives us time to adjust our eyes to the illumination.

Unity of spirit is not a scientific thing—it's of our spirits. Anniversaries are also not a science thing. There is no material meaning to a week's anniversary—a week being a human construct. The same is true for a daily anniversary—sunset. It's an artifact of the current speed of earth's rotation on its axis and around the sun, where you happen to be sitting on the planet, how many suns are in our vicinity (in our case, one), and even what wavelengths of electromagnetic radiation our bodies respond to. If we ran on gamma rays, we would not be quite so obedient to the sun's location and whether the earth is between it and us. The earth's position at midnight this coming December 31 is nowhere close to where it was on that date in 2007, let alone 1908.

All of these arbitrary things are not arbitrary because they are shared among our extended human community. We bring meaning to them. I hope I'm not the first to tell you there's really no Big Dipper up there, Southern Cross, Seven Sisters, or Orion's Belt. The stars appear in random positions that our brains bring order and meaning, to. But those shared, self-imposed illusions have created a heritage of story and philosophy among people over millennia.

All of which is to induce you to wrench unity from Hillary,

Barack, and New Hampshire, and invest in a little of our own.

This Thursday evening, July 10, is the three-month anniversary of the last interactions Nancy had with the world the rest of us continue to dwell upon. We had planned our day for Friday, gone to sleep at sunset as usual. Friday morning, only one of our crew awoke. Since then, I mark every Thursday evening/ Friday morning with a candle and a prayer. I doubt it does much for Nancy—I indulge myself.

So on this special, albeit arbitrary, confluence of the day, of the week, and of the month, all of us having experienced ninety degrees of earth's rotation around our sun (three months) of life without Nancy, maybe you'll join me in a little metaphysical unity. Assuming you're not sitting on an airliner or too close to a Holiday Inn Express smoke detector (they're sensitive—take if from me), at your own local sunset, please consider lighting a candle and investing a thought or a prayer in our shared companion. Candles have a lot of meaning, and thought is a powerful thing. Do yourself a favor and don't just think about it. Actually realize the ritual in material stuff—a match, a candle, a word spoken out loud.

Another powerful thing is music. Last Thursday I was riding home watching our solitary, mainly optically, luminescent sun's illusion of approaching the terrestrial optical phenomenon we refer to as a horizon. I was wondering if I'd be home before the two illusions coincided because it was the cue for me to light my candle and create the illusion of life in its infinitesimal smallness and fragility.

Do I think on the bike? No. It is the lack of thought I achieve on the bike. While I am not thinking, I try to wrap my brain around life's elements, especially Nancy. Mental state aside, I was listening to Jet's Shine On, one of my favorite CDs. It occurred to me, before the vocals even started (I've heard it so many times)—these are the words Nancy would be saying to me. Candles, sunsets, and anniversaries speak to most of us. If you get a chance, add Jet's Shine On (preferably the full length version that's on the CD, not the radio cut), to your ceremony this Thursday. I will.

Creation

August 22, 2008

Having grown up in the Midwest and spent a few weeks a year staying with my grandparents in Lima (where I visited my grandmother, Liesl, yesterday en route home from the West), I spent a lot of time in close range of cornfields. In the sixties, I used to ride to there—Tom and I tried to do it in one day but never succeeded. It's almost a hundred and fifty miles, which is a long way for two young kids on heavy Schwinn bikes.

Anyway, over many hours in the back seat of my grandparents' big American cars and on bikes riding country roads with farm crops growing much taller than I could see over, I developed my cornfield analogy. Imagine a space alien (S.A.) looking down at earth from a hovering UFO—maybe five miles up. S.A. would possibly see cornfields as groups of individuals. They are clearly populations of similar, but not identical, live beings. They appear certainly alive, and have several stages of life. And they live all over the country, in big cities, Iowa and Ohio farms, and small towns. I used to grow a few in our back yard in

Cleveland in a garden along with beans and other easily grown stuff.

S.A. has it about right—corn does require a village, at a minimum; it is alive; and it has a distinct life cycle. And no two are alike. Some are big and strong and dominant of resources; most just get by. Some are outliers on the edges of the field or even germinating far from the field, while others are central. Most are surrounded by others. Some grow large ears, some none.

Now imagine I am S.A. and corn is all the people around me. Therefore, I am both observer and part of the observed population. As S.A. (who through this new lens is a human being), I certainly find it far-fetched that every one of these corn plants has an individual soul, an immortal soul, and will die, only apparently to me as its observer, in fact, will live forever with its corn neighbors in a heaven inhabited by God, His minions, and corn angels. Presumably no corn-blight organisms go to heaven, or if they do, it's their own heaven, separate from corn heaven. What about Indian corn—the colored kernels— in fact, there are hundreds of strains of corn—are they all in one heaven? Or multiple heavens? Can they visit each other? Sometimes Indian corn is mixed in with white or yellow corn. Presumably, they interact in life—so how about in death? And the bees that pollinate the corn? They could be admitted, but in heaven corn doesn't need pollination, so no bees either—again, presumably they have their own bee heaven somewhere else.

Clearly, this is all pretty absurd. So how about cats and my beloved dog Windsor, Scotty before her, and the poor robin I killed with a BB gun, thinking I could never hit it, and even if I did, nothing would happen? We buried Ms. Robin in our back yard, and I made a tombstone for her with my wood-burning set. Surely Scotty would have a heaven—she died, drowned really, in my lap in the back seat of my mom's car as we raced to the vet—she was beyond old and had advanced COPD (Chronic Obstructive Pulmonary Disease). Ever since then, I've had a phobia of drowning. Surely brave Scotty is in a heaven for dogs? How else can I believe in an afterlife for myself—one devoid of Scotty?

But if Scotty is in heaven, then why not robin? And if robin, why not the flies? I went through a long period as a child befriending house flies—which I later believed might have had something to do with dermal warts I suffered with, but who knows? Maybe not. In any case, if flies, how about ants, which I also protected and still don't kill if avoidable, and ditto spiders? And is corn not as smart as an individual ant? Plants are really pretty clever, but that's another subject.

My mother tells me that the reason my brother and sister were December babies, but I'm a Virgo, is that a previous version of me miscarried, and rather than miss a year, my parents elected to try again immediately. So how about my unborn sibling? Did he or she qualify for human heaven? And when did the doors of human heaven open—I mean, in the evolutionary sense? Did proto-humans, pre-Homo sapiens, get in? And who decides when the first one got in? What about his parents, who presumably after a few billion years of evolution, were born fifteen years before the official start of the Homo sapiens era? That first one of us doesn't get to see his or her parents in Homo sapiens heaven? And no dogs in our heaven? So what about Scotty and me? I have to believe God can work these things out, since I can't. But then, I couldn't design a star or even a leaf, but He can, so presumably all these problems are solvable by God.

But for right now, what's our Space Alien, S.A., to make of all this? S.A. doesn't talk to people, corn, flies, birds, dogs, or spiders. S.A. talks to other S.As, whom he presumably cares about and believes will live forever in heaven, and he'll join them there at his end.

Where does this lead us? To a nowhere that is pretty much where all this sort of speculation leads. Spending enough time on a bicycle in the Midwest, one is forced to become a Ghandian, a Nihilist, or possibly a Jew.

Rabbi Roger Klein teaches courses as part of his work at The Temple in Cleveland, where my mother is one of his students. Through her, I recently had the opportunity to exchange some emails with him. Like medicine, though we don't like to admit it, a lot of religious and spiritual leadership happens nowadays via the Internet. Rabbi Klein, whom I have met only briefly during visits to Cleveland for family occasions, generously offered this sermon, which I can only describe as transcendental, from the High Holy Days of 2007 for publication as part of this book.

NEVERTHELESS ...

Rabbi Roger C. Klein
Yom Kippur
22 September 2007
10 Tishri 5768

I want to tell you something about what it's like being a rabbi, day in and day out, week in and week out. So much of it is filled with stimulation and joy: standing before you like this on Shabbat and holidays, sharing intimately your moments and seasons of happiness—baby namings, B'nai Mitzvah, weddings, anniversaries; studying Judaism's great texts and together drawing insight and practical wisdom from them; deepening friendships over the course of many years ... all this makes me realize how lucky I am to be your rabbi.

But there is another side to the life of a rabbi, and that is all trepidation and pain and grief that I witness and experience along with you. Talking with individuals torn up about their lives, speaking with parents worried about their children, meeting with husbands and wives distressed about their marriages, sitting at bedsides in homes and in hospitals at times of serious debility, seeing the prolonged illnesses and senseless deaths of people cut off before their time, feeling the pain and loneliness of the dying, trying to comfort families when their loved ones die. To witness the unavoidable sadness of living and to feel, over and over again, the fear and pain and despair of people I care about and love ... this causes my heart to ache. And, when experiences like this pile up with unusual frequency and intensity, as they have in recent months in our congregation, it produces in me a response which sometimes surprises me: I want to cry out, as you do, "Unfair, unfair!" And then I remember something the great American novelist, Annie Dillard, wrote about an experience she had one Sunday morning in church. "Once," she writes, "in the middle of the long pastoral prayer of intercession for the whole world—for the gift of wisdom to its leaders, for hope and mercy to the grieving and pained, succor to the oppressed, and God's grace to all—in the middle of this [the minister abruptly] stopped [in mid-sentence] and burst out [impatiently], 'Lord, we bring you these same petitions every week!'" (*Holy the Firm*, p. 57f.).

And this is how I sometimes feel: "Lord, we pray for health and people do not get better. We offer heartfelt petitions, but they fall on deaf ears. We ask, 'Why?' and we get no answers." And then I question whether life makes sense, whether there is order in the world or meaning in the human condition. I feel privileged to be involved in real life but real life hurts all too often. And so, at this time of year, and especially *this* year, I have been reflecting yet again on these questions and seeking a response that will help me and will perhaps help you, though responses that flinch from the truth or engage us in mere wishful thinking will be of no help to me whatsoever.

One of my brothers recently sent me a story about the famed violinist, Itzhak Perlman, which reads as follows:

One night "Perlman came on stage to give a concert at Lincoln Center in New York City. [For him], getting on stage is no small achievement ... He was stricken with polio as a child, and so he has braces on both legs and walks with the aid of two crutches. To see him walk across the stage one step at a time, painfully and slowly, is an awesome sight. He walks with great difficulty, yet majestically, until he reaches his chair. Then he sits down slowly, puts his crutches on the floor, undoes the clasps on his legs, tucks one foot back and extends the other foot forward. He bends down and picks up the violin, puts it under his chin, nods to the conductor and proceeds to play. By now, audiences are used to this ritual.

But this time, something went wrong. Just as he finished the first few bars of the concerto, one of the strings on his violin broke. You could hear it snap—it went off like gunfire across the room. There was no mistaking what that sound meant, and there was no mistaking what he had to do. He would have to stop, get up, put on the clasps again, pick up the crutches and limp his way off stage—either to find another violin or else to find another string for this one. But he didn't. Instead, he just sat there, waited a moment, closed his eyes, and then signaled the conductor to begin again.

The orchestra started up, and he played from where he had left off. And he played with such passion and such power and such purity as they had never heard before. Of course, anyone knows that it is impossible to play a symphonic work with just three strings. I know that and you know that, but that night Yitzhak Perlman refused to know that. You could see him modulating, changing, and recomposing the piece in his head.

When he finished, there was an awesome silence in the room. And then people rose and cheered from every corner of the auditorium.

Later backstage, Perlman was asked how he managed to pull off that astonishing feat. "You know," he modestly replied, "sometimes it is our task to find out how much music we can still make with what we have left."

And this is what I want to consider with you now: how much music can we still make with what we have left after we have been wounded by life? What resources do we have that can help us live energetically and purposefully?

The twentieth-century American poet, e.e. cummings, in his masterful and moving autobiography, presents glimpses of his mother, who, in his own words, was "the most amazing person I'd ever met":

> "... never have I encountered anyone more joyous, anyone healthier in body and mind, anyone quite so incapable of remembering a wrong, or anyone so completely and humanely and unaffectedly generous [as my mother] ... The two indispensable factors in life, my mother always maintained, were 'health and a sense of humor.' And although her health eventually failed her, she kept her sense of humor to the beginning" (*i: six nonlectures*, page 11f.).

"She kept her sense of humor to the beginning." This magical sentence describes, with stunning directness and brevity, the power of a sense of humor. Now, a sense of humor, in this conception, is not about telling jokes well or laughing at jokes readily or facilely turning out humorous asides. This way of understanding a sense of humor refers not to a set of activities *within* life, but rather, to a perspective *about* life. The seventeenth-century philosopher, Francis Bacon, captured the point perfectly when he said, "Imagination was given to man to compensate him for what he is not; a sense of humor to console him for what he is." With a sense of humor we face and acknowledge the tragedies and perplexities of life; by poking fun at them, we achieve some distance from our troubles and thereby neutralize some of their sting.

Two Jews were witnessing the funeral procession of Lord Rothschild. One of them was crying uncontrollably. "Were you then related to Lord Rothschild?" the other asked. "No," replied the first, "that's why I'm crying."

A sense of humor inoculates, though it doesn't cure. To be able to laugh at our condition and to find humor in our circumstances is to prepare ourselves to go on with our lives with sobered vitality, but with vitality nevertheless.

The realism and distancing offered by "keeping our sense of humor to the beginning" is the first in my proposed arsenal of responses to life's troubles. The second is the cultivation of optimism. I say "*cultivation* of optimism" because being optimistic in our world takes a deliberate and sometimes mighty effort. Optimism cuts against the grain of the way things are. But we must cultivate it nevertheless, or we will shrivel up and die.

An important example of this cultivation of optimism against the grain is the prayer we read during a funeral at the open grave of a loved one. The prayer reads as follows: "The Rock [that is, God], His work is perfect and all his ways are righteous. A faithful God and without iniquity, just and right is He." When I read this over the open grave ... and especially when the deceased has suffered terribly or died much too soon ... I have the feeling that I am saying something blasphemous, for no sentiment seems further from the truth at this moment than "the works of God are perfect and all his ways are righteous." And, as I read this prayer, I say to myself, "How can I utter this in front of these deeply wounded mourners because it seems to mock them and belittle their overwhelming sense of life's unfairness?" But in spite of my qualms, I do read it ... and I read it with conviction ... because I think I see what the prayer is aiming at. Here's what I imagine the author of the prayer would say about its meaning: "I know very well that the passage is descriptively false in significant ways.

And I know that it is just at times like this that the world looks deeply flawed and irrational, far from perfect and just and fair. But that's just the point. I wrote this passage to help people resist the descent into despair, and I do this by telling the mourners something they regard as preposterous but which is also true ... that the world is also beautiful and orderly and hospitable to human striving and that not every moment is like this moment. I tell them, in advance of their desire to do so, to look for what's good and promising in life and then to go after it and celebrate it and act *as if* there is a benevolent God and that 'all His works are perfect.'

And when the mourners return to the house of mourning, they will find waiting for them some of the things that make life good ... family and friends, love, home, food, sympathy, hope." And now, speaking in my own voice, I want to say that if I had the opportunity to raise my children all over again, the things I would try hardest to instill in them are the "habits of optimism" and the courage to make all the music they can with whatever they have left.

The consolations of humor and the optimism of hope ... to be expressed now, today. And here is the third in my proposed arsenal of responses to life's troubles. Don't we see that every moment provides an opportunity to learn something new, to touch another person, to deepen a friendship, to offer a smile, to make a difference in our community, to celebrate life? Abraham Joshua Heschel has fashioned a word that I love: the "herenow." Our emphasis, he says, should not be on the hereafter but on the herenow"... eternity is not perpetual future but perpetual presence." ("Reflections on Death," *Conservative Judaism*, Fall 1973, p. 9). The moments we have are gifts, and gifts are brought to fruition only when they are used. And we can always take advantage of the moments we have, even when we have been assaulted by what T. S. Eliot calls "the anguish of the marrow ... the fever of the bone" ("Whispers of Immortality"). This is the meaning of the great "hineni," uttered by Abraham and Moses explicitly and indirectly by Ruth and Esther. "Here I am." I am present; I am ready to act and to make a difference now. And in making a difference to others, we take a step toward healing ourselves.

The fourth ingredient begins in the recognition that we are always making an impression on others, especially those who love us and care about us. We are always teaching by how we live our lives. It's an opportunity that never ceases as long as the breath of life is in us. Why not, then, be a positive example? Why not demonstrate how to live and how to think when life assails us? Why not put aside the suffering in order to show children and grandchildren and friends the way?

I am moved over and over again at the funerals I conduct, when a son or a daughter or a grandchild gets up and says, through choked-back tears and halting sentences, how deeply affected they have been by the example of their parent or grandparent: "She didn't complain." "He always looked forward to tomorrow."

"He always asked how *I* was doing rather than dwelling on *his* pain." "She lived her life to the moment she died." This is something we should never forget: somebody's life ... our child's, our grandchild's, our friend's ... can be exalted by the way in which we live our lives.

A sense of humor, a cultivated optimism, living in the herenow, being a positive example for someone else ... these are the things which can help us live richly and well and which can fend off the weariness and despair that threatens us from time to time. But let us note what these elements have in common: each of them is the product of a choice, a decision, a determination to live a certain way. There is nothing necessary or inevitable about foregrounding a sense of humor, of living optimistically, of finding what each moment makes possible, of taking seriously our capacity to be a positive example to someone else. We can always choose ... and it would be easier ... to dwell on the tragic, to take ourselves too seriously, to cultivate pessimism, to balk at what today makes possible, to squander our opportunity to teach through our attitudes and our deeds.

To live better requires an act of will, real courage, and real determination. It requires what I call "the heroic nevertheless." It goes something like this: *in spite of* the way the world is, and *in spite of* my suffering, *nevertheless*, I resolve to maintain my sense of humor, my optimism, my focus on the herenow and on how I can impact others positively. This "heroic nevertheless" will not eliminate the terrors of life or give us an answer to the question, "Why?" But when the world knocks us off our feet, in small ways and large, these are the resources we have, in time, to get up off the floor and to live fully and well.

e. e. cummings relates a story about the mother he loved and admired so much.

"My father and mother were coming up from Cambridge to New Hampshire, one day, in their newly purchased automobile—an air-cooled Franklin, with an ash frame. As they neared the Ossipees [mountains], snow fell. My mother was driving; and, left to herself, would never have paused for such a trifle as snow. But as the snow increased, my father made her stop while he got out and wiped the windshield. Then he got in; and she drove on. Some minutes later, a locomotive cut the car in half, killing my father instantly. When two brakemen jumped from the halted train, they saw a woman standing— dazed but erect—beside a mangled machine; with blood "spouting" (as the older said to me) out of her head. One of her hands (the younger added) kept feeling her dress, as if trying to discover why it was wet. These men took my sixty-six year old mother by the arms and tried to lead her toward a nearby farmhouse; but she threw them off, strode straight to my father's body, and directed a group of scared spectators to cover him. When this had been done (and only then) she let them lead her away.

A day later, my sister and I entered a small, darkened room in a country hospital. She was still alive—why, the head doctor couldn't imagine. She wanted only one thing: to join the person she loved most. He was very near her, but she could not quite reach him. We spoke, and she recognized our voices. Gradually her own voice began to understand what its death would mean to these living children of hers: and very gradually a miracle happened. She decided to live." (*i: six nonlectures*, pp. 11-13).

This is what challenges us ... today and all days. When real life overwhelms us, in large ways and small, and when we feel "What's the use?"... then we have the opportunity to live with a sense of perspective, optimistically and alert and awake and poised to act. But it requires a choice. It requires a "decision to live."

Amen

I Know. I Know.

It's a strange and somewhat interesting duality, to understand a syndrome, and simultaneously to live it. Specifically, I know that grief lasts a long time—in some sense forever. I know I'm far from unique, and I definitely do not feel life has treated me unfairly. The opposite—I don't know why it's treated me so well, though I wish I could say the same for Nancy. I'm definitely not complaining.

Grief has elements of manic depressiveness. When you're up, you feel you've come to terms with it, and life is regaining its natural rhythm. But unexpectedly, that feeling is replaced by its opposite. Not really a dark side—I still believe that grieving is a welcome emotion that somehow reassures us that we still have and honor that person who was lost to us. And it gives us depth as a human being, as my friend Steve says, "You are a more complete, stronger person having traversed the valley of the shadow."

I could have even predicted that after the expenditure of energy to pull the nanosatellite launch vehicle conference together at Brown last week, there would be a physical and emotional letdown. The weekend was peaceful, and I enjoyed it. I took a seventy-mile ride in the warm drizzle on Saturday. Sunday was sunny, and I did a one-hour kayak loop around the pond, then biked to the pool and swam my local triathlon.

One symptom I know I have is I can't sit around too long. I have to get out of the house after a couple of hours. Since the pool opens late on Sunday, I did the kayak thing more to get out than to commune with the reeds and birds, though I like doing that and getting a little salt water splashed on me. I watch the big motorboats scoot in and out of the breach way—on Sundays mostly families and couples going out to fish. Their wake rocks the kayak. I like being a cork in a rough sea—it's a good metaphor.

Monday, I had to be back at Brown early. I left at 6:30 a.m. to bike up there. Halfway there, I pass Nancy's and my favorite restaurant—Corner Tavern, which is so typically Rhode Island. It's moderately run-down, fifty percent bar, and the restaurant serves a mixture of seafood and comfort food. I liked the clear chowder, a RI specialty. We would split quahogs—ninety percent bread, ten percent clam—and Nancy would order something like baked stuffed lobster or some local fish—mostly for the stuffing, French fries, and as a nod to healthy eating, coleslaw. Or meat loaf with mashed potatoes. With the requisite Diet Coke—the cabernet of the working woman.

We used to sit across one of their aged wood tables in a booth near the back wall, decorated with faded photos of RI in the early twentieth century and the aftermath of the "big one"—the hurricane of '38—and hold hands. A middle-aged couple like any other in the Corner Tavern, corner of Route 2 and 138, Greenwich, RI, except for our lack of the local accent. You can only be a Rhode Islander if your grandparents chopped wood in Coventry or fished out of Galilee.

It's easy enough to describe the memories and the thoughts. It's harder, and in my opinion, not possible or productive, to describe the accompanying emotions. Suffice it to say, it's been a blue period. Those happen. Nobody lives without them. I had them in college, in Altadena, sometimes in a hotel room in Kuala Lumpur or Yavne in Israel or Shin Yokohama. They are a part of being a human, and if real life doesn't occasionally provide an opportunity to really feel what sadness is, that's a loss in itself.

Today I leave to spend one night with old friends in Manhattan. Normally, I wouldn't look forward to that—not so comfortable sleeping in a tiny guest room in an Upper West Side flat, sharing a bathroom, living on their schedule and without my normal surroundings, albeit only for a few hours. But I met André and Carla through Nancy, who met her when Nancy was CFO at the Kennedy Center and Carla ran the Lincoln Center finances—and we have always enjoyed each other. Two CFOs with eccentric husbands they could commiserate about. That must have been 1988—twenty years—when we all first met. Carla and André drove the round trip from The City in one day to be at Nancy's service, and I haven't seen them since.

Then I have business in New York and go back to VA for a week starting Wednesday night, the twentieth anniversary of AeroAstro. I feel like a positive alternative of George W. Bush. The exiting cappo, only in my case leaving a healthy, successful enterprise to my successors. But like Bush, in a way I don't care. It's history I can leave in my past. Nancy history is harder to put in the attic. None of this running around I really want to do, but getting out of the house daily has another overtone, a lower frequency spectral component, which is getting out of these surroundings for a few days, or a week, or two weeks in Rome. Somehow the mechanics of shifting location seem to bring real life to the foreground.

As a behaviorist, I figure what works, works, and I don't question why. Not that there aren't hypotheses to why, and sometimes the search itself shines some light. But there are no answers to why, so I can abandon that search if it doesn't appeal to me. Like living with a dog or cat, the human should keep in mind, at least most of the time, who is the management.

—Rick

Life After Love

Steve,

I haven't read the book, but listened to this interview of the author of "Life After Love" on this author's life after the death of her husband. http://www.onpointradio.org/shows/2008/09/life-after-love/. Since you work in the hospice area (one of your many part-time jobs), I thought you might find it interesting, or maybe redundant. At the very end of the interview, there was a statement by one counselor that was new to me, though probably not to professionals. He said, more or less, "The death of a parent is the loss of the past. The death of a child is the loss of the future. The death of a spouse is the loss of the present." I haven't personally experienced the first two, except through friends who have, and this struck me as a simple and helpful idea to keep in mind.

We all have pasts, presents, and futures, and it is helpful to realize that while the loss of any one is not a desirable situation, the other two can be relied upon—a sort of partial redundancy, like having two eyes. Vision is better with both, but workable with one. Life rests on a tripod of these three eras. The analogy manifests when people offer hope that memories might comfort one who has suffered a loss. They are focusing on one of the remaining eras. Balance is trickier on a two-legged stool, but what I see in many others is it can be learned over time.

—Rick

Two Thoughts

Here are my two thoughts at the end of my weekly Nancy sabbath. I've never had a whole lot of enthusiasm for the Sabbath—one day free from work, and spend it in quiet contemplation? I enjoyed it in Israel because the lack of commercial activity (e.g., the malls are closed) actually forces people to see each other and not shop. As a person who doesn't like to shop, I liked that, but if shopping were the way I liked to relax on my day off, I probably would have avoided Israel with gusto. It's bad enough to work their hours all week, but then to have a day off prevented from enjoyment is not for me a Sabbath.

I now think this is another example of worshiping the ladder in the Sufi sense. Religion is a ladder we climb to give us a better view—a vision of what creation, what life is. While people argue that science and religion are not compatible, or fight wars over which religion is "right," if you see religion as a ladder, you realize that there are many different ladders, or towers, or telescopes, erected all over the world, and now in orbit around the earth too. Each of them has in common with the others that they help us to see better, further, more. The value of that extension of our consciousness explains the popularity of ladders and telescopes, and also of religion. The trouble, Sufism teaches, is that most people forget about the view and end up worshipping their ladder. The Sabbath as practiced in Orthodox Judaism is to me a version of worshipping the ladder.

Nancy and I used to argue the ridiculous point of what the imagery of the Sabbath Bride meant. It meant nothing to me—I didn't understand the Sabbath as a bride concept. But the point of it is—one welcomes the Sabbath and looks forward to it. I can't think of too many people who welcome and look forward to twenty-four hours of rules, regulations, and prohibitions on their actions.

My weekly practice is something I look forward to, and I'm wondering if you might add it to your repertoire of ways to help a family of a loved one in hospice. It's not helpful to grieve twenty-four/seven. Of course, grieving people feel it's not a choice. You go to bed grieving, grieve in your sleep, and wake up miserable. But at some point those feelings alleviate for short intervals. When that happens, your reaction isn't relief; it's guilt. That person is no less dead—they aren't getting better—and here you are enjoying life occasionally. In twenty-four/seven grieving, you are with the dead person—you are both one hundred percent immersed. In eight hours per day of normalcy, you are having more vacation from the loss in one day than your loved one will have for eternity. You have to face the fact that you can't "be there" for a dead person. They are in the being dead state, and you are still in the being alive state.

So now you have a double loss—you don't have the person anymore, and you are living with the pity for them. That's loss number one. Now, you perceive "recovery" as a loss of solidarity with that person. You are abandoning them and going about your merry way—enjoying food, friends, and work and, let's say, bicycling, to pick an arbitrary example. A bad thing happened, and to make things worse, you are turning your back, at least sometimes, on the whole thing.

My Nancy sabbath helps me deal with both of the losses. When I was in Italy, the work was very intense. Rushing to get going in the morning, busy all day, return to hotel late and tired. No time for reflection. And I do feel guilty if I go through a whole day without thinking of Nancy. Irrational? Yes, but real just the same. Therefore, I say to myself, life is what it is—it's not for me to call it wrong or right. It doesn't always make room for reflection and empathy. Sometimes surviving the day is its own victory.

We don't have control. But I tell myself—on Thursday evening, no matter how late I get in, I will reserve the energy and mental focus to think about Nancy, and not just her, but the whole experience and what it means to me at this moment. And I will reserve times during the day on Friday. You know, even if you have to work on your birthday, it's still your birthday in your own mind, and you celebrate it internally even if you can't be on the golf course or whatever. That's how I think on Fridays. It's Nancy's and my day, even if I'm speaking, meeting, teaching, or negotiating.

This is tremendously helpful. It gives me license not to grieve twenty-four/seven. I am not disloyal, because I have created discrete space. It would not be reasonable for that space to be one hundred percent of my time. One day out of seven goes all the way back to the Torah—if it has been good enough for almost six thousand years, who am I to argue with the ratio? If I'm at home, I have my candles and my prayers to read, but I'm not a ladder-worshiper. It would cheapen the whole thing if it were all about the ladder—the devices and places. I can't really control that—I control my thoughts, and that's what matters.

It helps me, and I figure there's nothing unique about me in the world of loss. Maybe it would help others to think in terms of a weekly day of remembrance, of contemplation and of learning.

Dedicate your private thoughts of that day to that person and all they meant, all they taught you, special words they said you want to remember, or where you were two, five, ten years ago at this time. Whatever you like—it's all kosher if it is your way of investing a day in thought.

Okay, thought du jour number two is shorter. When I'm at home, I read the Mourner's Kaddish twice a week—Thursday evenings and Friday mornings, and sometimes Friday evenings, too. Certainly, in part, for ritual, but in part to figure it out. It's like figuring out a boulder—what's it doing there, what's it made of, how did it end up where it is, and what is it trying to tell me? Maybe nothing, and I'm reading all that into the boulder. But man learns from boulders, and the more we learn, the more they teach us. We go all the way to Mars just to look at boulders. We spend billions of dollars to learn from boulders. Crazy.

Back to the Kaddish. First of all, like a boulder, it just is. It makes no claims. It asks nothing of the reader. It doesn't tell you how to act or what to think. It isn't Dr. Phil giving you little tools to get through the day. Unlike religion and philosophy, it's not a way of viewing loss or anything else. It doesn't invest in imagery—it doesn't say death is a horizon. It doesn't say anything about death, so avoids telling you the dead person is with God. Or not.

On the other hand, like a boulder, the Kaddish just is. It states what just is. What is it that just is? God is sort of the definition of the word "is." Like a boulder, the statement of the Kaddish is "is." You look at the entire natural world. Whatever your theory is about planets, stars, birds, glaciers, oceans, or atmospheres, the fact that you are theorizing about them means one thing for certain—they exist. Maybe not the way you think. For instance, we talk about quarks—little particles that are mixed together to make electrons and protons—and maybe they really don't exist. But at least as a philosophical construct, quarks exist just as much as justice or love.

There appears to be advice from the boulder known as Kaddish. It tells us to take the position that existence is a good thing, to be praised. Yes, we, as substantive things, exist in a world of substance, and few would argue against the wonder and the benefit of "is." So what first appears as advice—to praise God—is not advice. It is pure logic. "Is" existence, is a miracle of which we are one result, and everything we can ever experience or know or dream of—it's all a result of "is." Ultimately, that's what boulders tell us—that they are. They force us to realize their existence and induce us to wonder about it. The Kaddish is the same—it states the "is," and in just doing that, makes us wonder about and appreciate the miracle of existence.

Most poetry isn't really poetry—it's prophecy, or preaching, or story-telling. Modern poems are mostly cryptic short stories. They don't float above life—they are just a different style of everyday literary discourse. The Kaddish may be the only pure poem. It doesn't tell a story, doesn't preach, and doesn't "go anywhere." Made only out of words, it just is. There's nothing bigger than that—it contains everything else.

When Is Long Enough?

Friday morning—how many weeks has it been? I don't count anymore—enough weeks that one more week is not fifty, twenty-five, ten, or even five percent more time to accept. I'm living a normal life in the outside world, enjoying maybe more than ever the simple facts of existing and doing.

My father, not given to dressing up anything, responded to great synagogues, soaring churches we'd visit in Europe, and lavish funerals of politicians, that people look for God too far away. I, Survivor, find God in every thread of a favorite T-shirt and in the cat licking my toes when they first reach the carpet at 3:45 a.m. God is no more close to us at the pulpit or in the bell tower, in an airplane or in orbit, standing on the moon, or en route to the stars. We find God wherever we look for Her. And the meaning of life? *Lo stesso!* It's not in our *Meisterstück* anymore than in stepping outside in predawn and visiting the Milky Way and Greece's ancient constellations, or drinking a cup of hot bitter cocoa.

A swimming pool may be the ultimate in boredom, a readily available sensory deprivation chamber. And there I am, fully engaged, floating in a streamline on its surface, unconnected to morphine pumps, dilute IVs, moving without pain. If it makes you happy—that's what Cheryl Crow says. If it makes you happy to feel alive climbing a mountain or riding twelve hundred kilometers across the Pyrenees—go for it. However, there is no higher form of human life there than in a good day at work or running errands. It's all a miracle.

There is passion and there is compassion—passion without the sugar coat of reciprocity. If what we seek from life is passion, then we need the accomplishment of some objective to feed back to us, "You have lived." Ribbons, medals, diplomas, paychecks, cars, homes, clothes, and today's highest form of recognition—fame. We are told how strong the human drive is for acceptance in our groups. It's the carrot hanging on the stick two feet in front of our eyes. My advice? Every so often, forget passion—compassion is more rewarding. Lose the carrot, and the stick, the plow, and the field. Not forever—acceptance and success are worth some effort. But there's more out there, out of sight of that carrot right in front of us.

Love the ordinary—that doesn't broadcast back to you the accomplishment. Of feeding the cat, doing a day's work unappreciated and even unnoticed. Of putting away the groceries and cleaning up the kitchen or the bathroom. The everyday is the opportunity for compassion for God's creation and for your existence. Those special days—cruising into Rome after four long, cold, wet, and mountainous days on the bike—that's the passion of accomplishment, achievement, and admiration from those who would never try it, and wonder if you are amazing or deranged. We all need and deserve a few moments of pure passion—that's why it's there. But if it defines us, we are either hollow, or it will collapse. A simple, unappreciated task done out of compassion for the world, specifically without recognition, and to see in that invisible effort our reflection, which for a few moments we create within it, can bear your whole weight, even in grief.

Now that it's "long enough," I wonder—when will I be able to be alone—in the pool, on the bike, in bed at night, and not replay those memories I thought would have faded by now?

Holding Nancy's tray of crushed ice and juice, pausing outside her bedroom, hearing her tell Anita, her mother, "I'll end up just like Daddy." Daddy, the aerospace engineer who worked on the Northrop Flying Wing in WW II, who traded a career in engineering for Harvard Medical School. The powerful, athletic surgeon. Six feet tall, tennis player, runner, driver of BMW Bavarias, founder of a surgical practice in Southern California. The unquestioned master of the household—feared and beloved. Frozen in Nancy's high school memory was Daddy breaking a bone swinging a golf club, the first symptom of a rare bone cancer that emaciated him to the same place Nancy was that evening, her mother at her bedside, denying that history must inevitably repeat itself.

Daddy, who died in his tiny bedroom at home in Encino after months of decline, children and mom taking shifts caring for him, administering morphine. and feeding him juice and ice. Daddy couldn't beat it—why would Nancy be able to do what he couldn't? Hadn't he been her God?

Anita and I sat just outside the event horizon of our domestic black hole as Nancy spiraled gradually in. From bedside card table chairs, we denied history, physiology, gravity. We denied the rain, the wind, and the change of the seasons. We denied the day turning into night. Nancy, as was her way, wasn't buying our rationalizations. Maybe there is something that crossed that gravitational boundary to travel around and around with Nancy as she circled the invisible center. That something is what is real, what is blind to ourselves and our need to deny for our collective sake. Compassion.

Courtesy David Ascalon of Ascalon Studios

David and Goliath

Cures for
Jellyfish Stings

I have only my own childhood and only one brother as a sample set, but that unscientific basis has not deterred me from a simple conclusion—brothers fight, and not just when they are six and four years old. It's a lifestyle choice. Tom and I enjoy the adrenaline rush of potential annihilation just as much fifty years later as we did then. The difference is only that we now don't wrestle each other to the living room floor and slam doors in each other's faces. We've learned more subtle and effective techniques.

A few years ago, I was at a launch prep meeting at NASA KSC— Kennedy Space Center in Southeast Florida. It was never the toughest duty staying in the pre-Apollo era, and I've never upgraded from the Holiday Inn Cocoa Beach. (Notice how much classier that sounds than Cocoa Beach Holiday Inn, which would imply just another hotel in Cocoa). As the song said, "It's only words." Fact is, the HICB is the only place on the beach with rates as low as the government per diem. You can choose between going deaf via the whining of the air conditioner grinding its shot motor bearings, to dust all night, or prop the door open and sweat while the mosquitoes feast on your ears. But after a hot and sweaty day in meetings and maybe crawling around the shuttle bay, you can slip into running shorts, get even hotter and sweatier running on the beach, and then dive into the Atlantic, which makes the rest of the Holiday Inn experience totally worth it, to me, anyway.

That day a solid east wind had been blowing. I was in the water only a few minutes when I realized my skin was tingling. After a few minutes more of swimming and thinking about the strange sensations, I realized why—jellyfish. Lots of them. My arms and legs were covered with red streaks.

I made an adrenaline-fueled sprint back to the beach, ran up to the hotel, and jumped in the freshwater pool, hoping to wash off some of the toxin. I then retreated to my room and the company of my body's reaction to my potentially anaphylactic swimming companions. Things were looking and feeling genuinely painful by then. My skin was burning, itching, red, and swollen all over.

I was panicked. I know about as much about medicine and first aid as your average man on the street knows about building microsatellites, which is to say nothing. It occurred to me to call my brother, Tom. Granted, he's an orthopedist and doesn't treat many patients with toxic marine creature encounters, but I figured he had to know more than I did. Should I head for the ER stat or get ice, antihistamines, steroidal skin cream, soap, or maybe some topical alcohol? I have no clue, but am beginning to wonder if I'm going to die in this little room.

This was way pre-cellphone. I had to dial into my Sprint account and then try Tom's numbers at work, get his answering service, and then his home. My fingers hurt just to punch the sticky buttons on the room's phone. I caught him just coming home from the hospital. I laid out my dire situation.

One nice thing about MDs is they mostly don't lecture you on what an idiot you are. I guess they realize their patient's idiocy is making their house payment. Or do they actually have pity on us unfortunates? Maybe they know patients will migrate to MDs who withhold truth in favor of dignity. I tend to doubt the more generous interpretation, but I was glad to get to the point and save the lecture for later, if I lived.

Tom starts rattling off advice. I have to get a pen and paper. He starts over—salt, alcohol, soap, salves, cotton gauze—all sorts of stuff. I have two hotel notepad pages of medications. I think I can manage putting on shorts and a T, and driving, though it's going to hurt. Toughing it out is one of my specialties. "Okay," I tell him, "I'll give it a try." I planned to hang up abruptly, anxious to get going before things got much worse.

"By the way, is this going to work? " I ask, while reaching for the phone's cradle. Tom is a man of few words.

"Just do it. Call me back later."

I'm out the door. Jump in the car. I stifle a desire to speed to CVS. I'm a manic man on a mission, scanning the shelves under the fluorescents. VISA card, keys, drive back. Pour most of my haul in the bathtub and soak in it for fifteen minutes. Then pat dry and apply the rest of the contents onto my wounded skin.

An hour later, fifty-five dollars poorer, wetter, drier, and now covered with creams, things are no better. But maybe no worse. I'm suffering, but I'm no longer as certain I will die before morning. I pick up the phone and call Tom with my update.

"Is any of this stuff really going to work?" Lacking relief, I'm desperate for reassurance.

"There really isn't anything you can do for jellyfish burns. But, by the time you make the list, run out to CVS, soak, dry off, and apply creams, it will start to go away by itself."

"You mean I could have skipped this whole exercise?"

Silence is his response.

"A shopping bag full of pharmaceuticals, an hour of running around, and an hour in the tub to learn 'Time heals all wounds'?"

My brother is clearly enjoying this moment of non-communication over the long-distance line. The great surgeon finally offers: "You'll be fine in an hour. Watch TV, go for a walk, soak in the tub, swim in the pool, and go buy vegetables or whatever it is you eat. Watermelon—if it makes you happy."

Score one for the big brother. I spend the next hour walking to Publix for a watermelon and a knife, planning my revenge. Maybe I'll save the knife.

Loved One Who Dies

When the person you love dies; there are so many things you can do—and I've done all of them. You can cry; get mad; light candles; write books; set up memorial funds; erect shrines; pray; talk with friends, families, counselors and clergy. You might read books on death and dying, go for long bike rides and walks, alone and with friends, or buy yourself something your loved one would have wanted you to have. You might invite everyone on the planet to a memorial service, sit in a room with all your loved one's stuff and recollect, have nightmares and dreams, or don't sleep at all. Get a dog or a cat; love the remaining people in your life more than you used to, challenge yourself with something new, try to appreciate life more than you used to, stop doing stuff you never wanted to do and start building a new life you like better, realizing this is the only one you've got. You might beat yourself up for being inadequate, or because you should have died instead. Play what-if games until you can't stand them anymore. Imagine you'll reunite with that person when you die (which does reduce the fear of death, at least one iota), speak with your departed (who won't answer), speak with your pet (ditto), sing out loud, set up a charitable fund in their name, put on your game face and go back to work, travel, throw yourself into projects, spend time alone, contribute to the departed's favorite churches and synagogues, or give all your loved one's stuff to the needy.

All this doing will take months, if not years, and it will be exhausting. Like treating jellyfish stings with alcohol, bath salts, creams and salves, bandages and pills, none of it works.

But it's something to do while time erodes the acute emotions into a palette that redraws your world in new, maybe darker, but also richer hues. You're not going to be eight Crayola colors anymore—you're more of a Rembrandt. You are being reborn—your old self died with that person, and neither of you is coming back. Your old skin is shed and everything hurts. New skin only grows back slowly, and for a long time it's thin and fragile.

No injury is fun, but its paradox is that when you heal to a certain point, your confidence blossoms. You walked through the valley of death, or in the case of injury, through pain and disability. And you survived and recovered, better than you thought you would.

Nobody thinks they have the strength, not that they'd want to try, and not that you had the choice. You're suffering, but you're keeping alive. You don't want to be happy, because your sadness is your memories, and you have every right to keep them and to celebrate them through a measure of misery.

It's bitter, but it's yours. Bitter can be nourishing too.

I never found happiness in a broken clavicle—a mere nuisance by comparison. However, you can find confidence in your ability to make that journey, and with a new you that can never arrive or go home again. You wonder if you will wander like a nomad without a country, possibly forever. You know what it is to be alive, to be human and to wander that desert. You now know our shared human condition.

Immortality is not a goal of mine, nor was it for Nancy. We both believe(d) in living as one visits a national park—leaving only footprints, if that. The Costume Fund was created in Nancy's name to provide a more meaningful way to pay a tribute to her memory than flowers. And many were generous in donating—both at her birthday in October last year, and after her death in April.

In consultation with Maryland Youth Ballet management, I have agreed to continue to spearhead that fund. With Nancy is its namesake, the fund's mission is to improve the experience MYB offers its dancers and audience. The art of ballet is more than dance. It encompasses music, choreography, and costume, both of specially made dance shoes and of handcrafted costumes. If you elect to donate to this year's drive, I hope you will do so to help MYB in its mission of service to young dancers and to ballet in the greater Washington area.

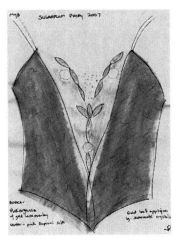

With this note are sketches of the new costumes the fund plans to support this year. They are beautiful, and will be especially welcome, given the age and condition of those they replace.

I hope you'll join me in supporting MYB and all the arts of ballet it preserves and refreshes by contributing to this year's drive. We are still accepting money the old-fashioned way. Please mail a check to:

Maryland Youth Ballet
926 Ellsworth Drive
Silver Spring, MD 20910
Specify: Nancy Fleeter Costume Fund

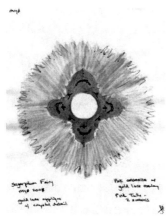

Each donor will receive a confirmation letter to document their donation both as a sign of our appreciation and for recordkeeping/tax purposes.

Thanks in advance for your continued support of MYB.

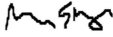

Rick Fleeter
Maryland Youth Ballet
Nancy Fleeter Costume Fund Chair
October 18, 2008

If God Exists

I thought I had read almost all the God quotes, but this one was new to me. It reminded me of when Peppermint Patty in Peanuts learned about Darwinian selection and said something like, "Who came up with THAT system?"

"I don't know if God exists, but it would be better for His reputation if he didn't."

~Jules Renard, writer (1864–1910)

Courtesy David Ascalon of Ascalon Studios

Jacob's Dream

Dreams
and Other
One-Way Conversations

Do the woods, the heavens, the sea, and the mountains speak to you? Does one city tell you it's welcoming you, another to be on your guard, and another lure you with special places yet to be discovered? Some bicycles beg me to ride them. Others say they are not for me. We all have clothes that we know are best for a wedding, a funeral, a job interview, or a special day outdoors with a friend. Cars speak to many of us—we choose one that appeals—like picking that one special puppy from a litter.

Here's a harder question: Do you talk back to the woods, sea, mountains, stars, bicycles, cars, dresses, shoes, and fish? Don't men yell at the television when their team's pass is intercepted just after the two-minute warning? I had a girlfriend who kissed, lips to lips (yes, fish have lips) her tropical fish every day when she came home after work. Her aquarium took up a good portion of her kitchen counter, and while she prepared her meals, she told her fish all about her day. It was sweet, maybe a little unusual. I admit to having a little trouble kissing her thinking about where her lips had just been, which, when you think about it, was no more rational than her kissing a fish who has been her companion for many years of living alone in an apartment in West Hollywood. Hey, lots of people talk to their plants, and some scientists think the plants do better for it.

How do you talk to the mountains as you hike their crevices and spine, ski down their snowy coats, or just watch the sunset turn their expanse of granite orange and then purple? I suppose there are people who actually talk out loud to what we call inanimate objects. But most of us speak to nature, to wild animals, even to our golf ball in midflight, or meandering more or less toward the flag, in our thoughts.

Point being, all our lives, since we cuddled a plush cartoon animal in our cribs, we have practiced relationships that are way outside the only conversation we actually call conversation—human to human in spoken language. If we kept track, we'd be surprised at how much time we spend talking to non-humans compared to humans. And I don't mean the turkeys sitting in the other cubes in your office. When we say our prayers, do the words actually reach God's ears, or is it only the act of prayer that increases the power of our thought and our faith?

How about our dreams? Don't they speak to us? People decide to get married, change careers, change their outlook, or confront their boss. Or they may do all sorts of important things because of a dream. We dream of flying, of dying, of places we've never been in our physical lives, of people we have no chance to actually meet or ever see again.

After Nancy died, the whispering messages of my dreams grew so loud they woke me up, a lot. For which I was thankful. She cried out to me to do something to save her. She appeared alive, well, and ready to participate in our life, except nobody else could see or hear her. She appeared only as a white-on-white sketch of herself, hovering over the scenes of my everyday life. In my dreams, Nancy blamed me for living. She went on vacations with me; she appeared as her dead self, still in her hospital bed the way I found her one early morning in springtime as the doves spoke to the setting moon outside her window.

Disturbing? I dreaded going to bed, because the dreams woke me up several times every night. These dreams were communications with the dead, but not the ones I would have hoped for. They echoed in my mind all day, especially during quiet times on the bike or in the pool. I knew, I believed, they were my own mind ruminating, but it didn't matter.

Unable to avoid them, I took up a new strategy. I would confront them. When they woke me up, I wrote them down on paper. I catalogued the dreams and asked myself, "What are they telling me?" I didn't always agree with Nancy—and I didn't have to agree with some of the messages of these dreams.

I could not accept blame for not saving her from cancer—I'm an engineer, not an oncologist. I cared for her for years. I pushed her to get the next opinion, try the next treatment, and never give up. She got mad at me sometimes for pushing so hard. Too hard. That guilt of occasionally making her life even more miserable I can live with. Yes. I plead guilty of that, and I'm proud of imposing my decision to accept more pain for the possibility of a gain. Letting her die was not in my vocabulary while she was alive, but it was in many dreams after she died.

It's no surprise I wanted Nancy to be alive and talking to me from her favorite docking station—the couch pulled up way too close to the screen of the big TV. Every survivor, even those who had mixed feelings during the life of the deceased, sometimes wishes their favorite irritant were at hand, if for nothing else than a good argument. Dreams are usually about the impossible. Starting with dreaming, we could grasp our pillow and fly over the landscape, soaring like a Red Hawk over a cornfield. Those escapes into fantasy are healthy, like stretching and yoga for the brain, and in their own way, so are these Nancy experiences. Death is a solid line, and dreams fuzz it out a little bit—so what? Either way, I'm making my way to its other side.

On this other side, I now know what the Bible means or what people mean when they say their loved one is alive in the meadows, the boulders, the good earth, the sky, and the sea. Some people spread ashes in these places. As a scientific type I don't get it. Ashes are carbon and calcium, regardless of whether those atoms might have spent a few hours or days in Nancy's body. They are no different from the calcium in a Rolaids tablet or a seashell. We don't know what stuff the soul is made of, but it's not likely to be a mixture of atoms in a jar. We might as well put air in the jar. There will be some atoms in there that Nancy once breathed in, that attached to her hemoglobin, that fueled her muscles and brain, and some that were exhaled attached to carbon. We breathe those atoms every day, as does every other person, animal, and plant on earth.

It's not about atoms. It's about relationships with what's on the other side of that line. Nancy can't talk to me as she did when she was a living person. Her communication to me is in the same language as my other constant companions—the endless stretches of black tarmac that keep me company while pedaling the countryside on my bicycle; the cold wind and icy black sky that greets me when I step outside on a winter night in New England; the snow that crunches under my boots as I trudge home from class late on a Thursday night in February, telling me about the season and the life I've chosen to live, for its better and its worse. That is how Nancy has joined nature. In my communication back to her, I don't talk to her in English or Spanish or Japanese, because, like many men, my emotions are well insulated from speech, eyes, and expression. I don't talk to boulders in poetic phrases, but I talk with my perception, with my ears, with my thoughts, what I can make of this world, what possibilities the open expanse of land or an image of a blank page on a computer screen present me for my expression. That's how I talk to Nancy.

I really don't get much comfort from asphalt, from a stuffed animal, from a fish, or from a beach, compared with having lunch with Nancy at her favorite Mexican place. But it's not zero either. We don't have the option to lunch together, to vacation in rural Italy, to share a ride home when the weather is too icy to bike and she's glad to turn over the wheel to the big lug who grew up in this absurd weather. And that leaves a big void.

We now know there is no perfect vacuum. Empty space is filled with cosmic rays, with dark energy, with electromagnetic fields, with particles, and with energy. It's a lively, crowded space, most of which just happens to be invisible to our eyes and ears, tuned as they are to the noise and light of our terrestrial environment. It's hard to grow a tomato or have a decent swim in space. However, we can do other things there, such as gather energy, learn about the nature of matter and the universe, travel at high velocity, and study God's mechanics at a grand scale. Some people's lives are totally consumed in that supposedly empty space. So how empty is it?

Death also looks dismal and empty. The conversations available to us are not audible to our logic, our language, our gestures, or our mainline ways of communicating. There's no touch, no smell, no taste, no sound. But neither is it empty. It speaks to us with the silence of the Grand Canyon at dawn. It is bigger than anything on earth, bigger than the sky, and it is with us every minute of every day. We go inside at night and avoid the voices of the sky, the cold air, the waves, and the traffic. Like a cosmic ray, death penetrates our homes, our offices, and our sleep. It is a constant companion. Its presence used to haunt me, but I have learned from its speech and from my backtalk, sometimes angry, sometimes wistful, usually plaintive and confused. I have learned to be grateful.

Helicopter Rescue

Besides avoiding death, being plucked from the side of a rock face in darkness at 11,700 feet altitude by a Utah highway patrol jet helicopter yields several other benefits. Among them is comfort, knowing that aerospace engineering, company management, and university teaching have been infiltrated by bureaucracy, along with a disembodied bureaucratic construct—"incident management"—for which there is a fee. Incident management, ephemeral though it may seem, nonetheless costs as much as the military trained pilot with forty years' rotary aircraft experience and his expert-trained search and rescue crew.

The cost of all this was a modest $1,190 fee for a helicopter, plus flight fees of $700 an hour and $240 for the helicopter crew. The helicopter crew consisted of a pilot, plus the guy who grabbed my arm while helping me leap off my rock perch onto the landing skid of the helicopter. When I pondered the complexities of leaping across the black hole of darkness, suddenly the rock perch seemed much more appealing than it did before help arrived.

But as my dad wisely pointed out, this $1,870 could have easily been spent just being rescued by ambulance and admitted to the Park City Emergency Room, and maybe getting a blood test, before the bill grew another several zeroes left of the decimal point with the addition of MRI, and ER docs, and nurses. And my bill would have gained yet another order of magnitude with surgery, follow-up therapy, and medical visits. In other words, a rescue is as expensive as a week's cycling vacation in the Alps or, taking the positive view, it may have saved me the equivalent of a retirement bungalow in the Ozarks. None of this counts the months of unproductive time that would have been spent in medical care, then in physical therapy, taking drugs, and hurting. Or worse.

Outside of existential issues, how was the hike? Rocky. From about the time we reached the bouldered semi-summit for lunch—way ahead of schedule despite climbing a lot of rock with no climbing gear and dressed in T-shirts and running shoes—and started down various nearly vertical walls and chimneys, I had cycled through all the modes.

First there was denying that it was going to be as bad as it in fact was, followed by bargaining: If I ever get off this mountain I'll stick to safer endeavors—like cycling to Tyson's II in Virginia on the shoulder of Route 7 with cars zooming past at 65 mph, or maybe cliff-diving in Monterey. I toyed with anger for a while, but getting mad at the only guy who has ever been there before seemed counter to my overarching goal of survival. (Though it turned out the guide never had been there before—so just as Seinfeld once pondered the definition of "reservation," I began to ponder the definition of "guide.") Finally I reached acceptance that this was a ridiculous situation. But unlike some situations, this one was completely curable if we made the right decisions, which included giving it the best try we could and then bailing if all else failed.

While the guide helped talk my left foot and then my right foot down long steps onto toe-width slivers of semi-horizontal rock, me facing the wall and gripping the cracks like they teach at Yosemite, I distracted myself thinking about my recent past.

I calculated that in the last twelve years I'd spent ten percent of my time in wheelchairs, casts, hospital beds, and crutches, recovering from bone breaks—three clavicles, two ankles, one shoulder, several ribs, and almost all the bones in one foot. Another ten percent of those years were spent caring for my wife, Nancy.

A business friend of mine is just now able to travel on crutches, months after breaking his leg while climbing. And a cycling friend has a chance to go home to a life of twenty-four/seven care in a few weeks following three months in the hospital, much of which time he spent unconscious due to a head injury. He may never be able to work or recover his personality.

Then I thought about a passage in one of the library of death and dying books I studied to help cope with Nancy's care. The author pointed out how hard people work, the lengths they go to, the money they will spend to save their life or that of a loved one. Yet the same person will put the whole enterprise at risk to save a few seconds at a red light, or to have a little fun on a weekend, or to share a drink with friends out for dinner. Okay, not the sort of thoughts to motivate a person to muster maximum gusto to make it through the next few hours.

The guide and I spent four hours sitting on our perch wondering if we were going to spend the night wrapped in a couple of rain parkas trying to sleep in twenty-degree air next to the burnt-out remains of the micro fire he built from the scant combustibles one can find on a rock outcropping. He had skittered around the rocks collecting what wood and boughs he could, but nothing that would do much more than briefly flare.

While the sun set across the valley we listened to the absolute quiet when the thermal-driven wind subsided and watched the stars emerge in a purple sky. We wondered what phase the moon would be in that night. We analyzed headlights on the road miles away to see if any looked like they were looking for us. We adapted, enjoying the strange uniqueness of our moment and its beauty. I remembered the last time I had slept outside—twenty-six summers ago rafting a California river. Camping, I confirmed at the time, was not my passion.

Then we heard the helicopter, but it didn't come near us. We thought he didn't see our little fire and our yellow and blue jackets draped over rock piles. In fact, we learned later, our fire was blindingly bright in the pilot's night-vision goggles. A few minutes later, the big rotating blades were on top of us, blowing embers from the fire onto our skin. Seconds later I was just a passenger in the back seat of a small aircraft making a short, comfortable flight to the same meadow the day had begun that morning.

Days later, ten minutes still don't pass without my marveling that I am not in a hospital, that all my limbs are in one piece, though my hands and legs are scarred from rock hugging. This year I watched a person gradually die, and I know what each of us really wants from life—the ability to enjoy it. The rest—our quest for fun, for experiences, for salaries, for a good watermelon, for a better-fitting cycling jersey, for the right stock buys, for all the things we tell ourselves matter enough to trade our time, maybe all of our time—is just details.

—Rick

September 9, 2008.
(From Anita, Nancy's mother)

Rick,

It has been a few days, but in the NY *Times* I read of a "rock-climber-hiker," also a mathematician/creative thinker kind of person, as you are, who tragically was climbing in Washington state and fell; perhaps you know of him. He left a family, and I realize I am being morbid, but I keep thinking what is it that makes gifted people take unusual risks. I have an old friend who still lives in San Diego, divorced her first husband, married a very gifted engineer/inventor type, and they traveled the world so he could skydive. He won many competitions, and it finally failed him.

Enough of that. In ten days I go to Pittsburgh to dance. That should be safe enough.

Love,
Anita

From Rick to Anita
I saw the article and sent it to my mom.

I think the differentiator is obvious. Smart people make more money than Joe Six-Pack and are more creative in how they use their spare time. Nobody slips off a mountain while watching their HDTV. They die of heart disease, diabetes, and strokes, and you don't read about them.

But having said that, risk-taking cuts across all income and intelligence levels. Look at the Harley drivers without helmets. Some people need that stimulation, as we've discussed. Those of us with life stories like yours and mine (and I include the risks associated with AeroAstro and my career choices in general, including what I'm doing now), tend to minimize controllable risk, which is why I opted for the helicopter rescue, which I think you read about.

I sent the obituary to my mom and dad—my point being that I took a lot of criticism on my blog about bailing on our "hike" when it clearly got too dangerous, despite the inconvenience and cost. I think I paid about $900 to be rescued, and the guide's company paid a similar amount. When I was a student at Stanford, I took a three-day rock-climbing course at Yosemite—considered among the best in the world, and I climbed in California as a means of getting over my fear of heights. It didn't really work, but at least I learned about something. One major lesson they teach is that people rarely get hurt on rock climbs with ropes and all the equipment if they're climbing in teams. They get hurt most often on casual hikes that are actually dangerous enough that the climbers *should* be using helmets, ropes, etc.

On our climb in Utah, which was supposed to be a simple hike, very quickly turned into serious climbing, and we were totally unprotected. Well, there's a lot of macho "I can do this" sort of attitude, and our twenty-one-year-old guide contributed to that, urging us on by saying we could do this and the end was in sight. Hey, I broke my pelvis falling off a bike just a few miles from home. Fate doesn't care. When I was a pilot, they taught us flights aren't over until the plane is tied down and you're in the office doing the paperwork, meaning, accidents happen in the parking lot, too.

I'll almost guarantee this death described in the article you sent was the same. I don't think the guy understood advanced climbing, and highly capable people tend to think, if others can do this, how hard can it be? That's how they attack tough problems. But in math, if you blow it, you crumple the paper up, and you've lost a day or whatever. In rock climbing, if you blow it, you end up like my officemate, Craig, with a smashed femur, or dead.

I figured, and my dad agreed. A thousand dollars is less than just the ambulance and ER fees. I thought it was a bargain, but the guide's boss yelled at me, "You weren't even hurt yet!" —implying I should keep pushing until an accident happens— and *then* call for help. What a nut!

—Rick

October 17, 2008
(From Susan)

Hi Rick,

I can't remember the date for sure, but I'm thinking Nancy's birthday is right around now. Hoping you are doing okay. We haven't communicated in a while. I know you've been various places. It has been a busy fall around here ... work and several quick out-of-town trips.

Hope to talk soon!
Susan

Rick's Reply to Susan

Hi Susan,

Only a few more people remembered that birthday, and probably some who do are reluctant to bring it up. You and I know better. It's the eighteenth—the first birthday she isn't here for. It reminds me of last year. Sheila and Ned came by, and the gift was the establishment of her costume fund at MYB, plus some champagne which she didn't feel was the best food for her, but she took a sip. It was in the days of the hospital bed, but she was still able to ambulate around the main floor of the house.

I think of that whole period like I think of college. A special time, but one I'm glad not to relive. Then we had hope, but each realized things were in a generally negative direction, and we knew no standard procedures were working. How I got through that, I don't know, nor how she did so well, but I'm glad to not have another year like that. As I said to my mother, one is forced to the conclusion there are situations worse than death.

What I see happening is that in my previous life Nancy and I were on a particular trajectory. As time passes, without any real planning on my part, that trajectory is slowly tailoring itself to a different life. The old trajectory got me to a certain location at a certain pace—let's say in the jobs I had, the real estate we purchased, cars, relationships with people, and possessions. Slowly those things are changing. It's almost like a magic hand is reshaping my life into one appropriate for a single person with a cat, rather than a married person with a combined plan. On the one hand it's logical enough, but it's still something I don't quite understand—how that happens.

A good marriage is like a comfortable shoe. It fits you, and you're glad to have it. It protects you from uncomfortable things, it makes walking—daily life—smoother, springier. But at the same time, it shapes your foot. My brother says a shoe is essentially a cast. When you shed that shoe, many things happen. For one thing, your foot changes shape. For another, you are a lot more susceptible to discomfort. Some people spend their whole lives barefoot; others are only barefoot occasionally. I'm not really sure one mode is preferable, but they are different.

To extend the metaphor, if you are barefoot long enough, your feet get tougher and stiffer. They become your own biological shoe. They have a shape; they offer some protection, maybe not as good as high-end New Balance. The differences may be smaller than you'd at first expect. What is at first a radical change slowly becomes the new normal.

—Rick

To Start off Your Week

I always wondered what the point was of keeping someone's cremated remains around. As a scientist, I don't put much stock in a few grams of oxidized minerals. Even in a spiritual sense, there is still not any way I can think those molecules of calcium carbonate are some essential part of Nancy.

What it does do for me, besides the urn's decorative value as the central element of my little Nancy memorial countertop space, is that the remains are a daily reminder of death's finality—of not to deny death. I believe more and more that denying the finality of death is a form of self-torture that bereaved indulge in because some part of us wants to be sad in solidarity with the person who died. Believing that some service is owed to that person imposes a burden, and at the same time denies that they are one-hundred percent gone. Even though it sounds hard and cruel, I think the hardest thing is to realize we do these things for ourselves and for the living among us. Unfortunately, the only alternative is to believe these habits are in some way a comfort to the departed person, which is a form of death denial. It's natural to deny death to avoid its being so cold and cruel. It's a dilemma, and the cremated remains in their little ceramic container force me to confront.

Not to resolve it, we agree there are no answers. But no answers doesn't equal no thinking is worthwhile. Some people believe in a continuing dialog with the dead person, and I don't mean with the elements of that person that live in them. I mean with that person. I'm not prepared to call them wrong, but I'm also not so quick to say that there's nothing. How would I know? What matters, I think, is to be conscious of the issues, and that urn and the ashes inside are the boulder that speaks to that subject.

Point two is that, whatever the literary elements of the Kaddish, I have to say that it's a great comfort when I'm going through a sad period, which I've had a lot of lately. It's good to be reminded that whether this world is perfect (and we just don't see the whole picture) or not, it is worthy of appreciation and praise, whatever our personal state of mind. This is not to put down the other psalms, though I find some of them much harder to interpret. Kaddish is simple, clear, and to the point. It doesn't decorate or embellish the death, and it is a helpful reminder to keep things in perspective. It reminds me that it's okay to feel sad, but it's also okay, in fact mandatory, to appreciate the world that I'm living in.

Only a Horizon

I admit I've overstudied death, dying, hospice, and all the issues that surround it. I feel like the old joke: Do you know the definition of a consultant? A guy who knows a hundred ways to make love, but has never had a girlfriend (thank you for that, Mark).

With that caveat, I found this short poem on the last page of a book on hospice care. My guess is ninety-nine percent of the people who have read the book never notice this page, which contains only this poem composed by Rossiter Worthington Raymond (1840–1918). He was, of all things, an engineer who wrote hymnals and a few fiction books as a sideline.

> Life is eternal, and love is immortal,
> and death is only a horizon:
> and a horizon is nothing save the limit of our sight.

Here's my interpretation.

A lot of people like to say that love never dies, or death is an illusion. I think that is wishful thinking and contrary to experience. It's a polite thing to say, but it offers little comfort, being obviously meaningless at best and wrong at worst. However, I also think Raymond knew what he was talking about.

Life is eternal with the capital L. He didn't start the poem with that word capitalized by accident. One individual's death does not end Life. Robert Frost said the one thing he could have learned about Life was that it goes on. Frost meant the life of animals and plants in general, the general notion of life, not a particular life small L.

Note that Raymond does *not* claim life is immortal. He leaves open the obvious truth that life by definition includes mortality. In a sense, we can define that which is alive by that which is capable of dying. Thus, we can safely say Life is eternal, but we can never say life is immortal. Mortality is a fundamental element of life. The two cannot be separated anymore than light and darkness. Without one, the other does not exist. Music is written on a canvas of silence. No silence equals no music. Life exists in its contrast to the backdrop of all that does not live or no longer lives. Life is clearly mortal.

By contrast, love, he says, *is* immortal. True on several levels. The death of a loved one does not end our love for that person. The person is mortal; the love for that person is immortal. Alternatively, for that matter, the death of a favorite artist, or even of a beloved dog or cat—our love for all of them survives mortality and death. Clearly, love keeps on beyond death and is in that sense immortal.

In a greater sense, love is a quality of sentient beings—people, but also probably many animals (I believe our dogs love us, and that calves are loved by their mother cows, for example). The death of any one person may only serve to strengthen the institution of love. Many people only realize love through death, so it truly must be immortal.

"Death is only a horizon"? Frankly, I question the word "only." Death may be more than a horizon. The word "only" is the assertion of the poem. The word "only" is the central theorem of his personal point of view; the rest of the poem is the frame around "only." So I can think about whether I agree with his "only," but still agree with the rest of the poem. I don't have to agree with everything Raymond says. Nor disagree. I am agnostic on "only."

But what about the idea of death as a horizon? Certainly it's a possibility, since by definition a horizon is two things—intangible and something beyond which we cannot see. You can't put a horizon in a zip-lock bag or any physical container; it is not a thing, or even a place. It is a phenomenon. You can't go to a spot and put a marker on the sea and say, "This is the horizon."

In addition, if you could see beyond it, then it wouldn't be the horizon.

Death is similarly intangible. We know it when we see it, but we cannot put a label on it, or put it in a box. It is a phenomenon. We can say, "This being has died," which is like saying England is beyond the horizon when I stand on Cape Cod. But death itself? It's like finding the horizon itself.

Finally, like the horizon, death is by definition that territory the living cannot see. Death is what living isn't.

And that leads to his conclusion. Death, that concept which above all others we fear, which we have to grapple with every day of our mortal existence, does not end Life, does not decrease, but actually may increase, love, and is made meaningful purely because of its mystery, its inaccessibility to the sight of the living. In a base sense, if we could talk to our dead uncle, death would be denied.

Death Is My Penpal

Until now, death was my one hundred percent the enemy. Now it is my ninety-nine percent enemy and my one percent friend. There really are times when death is preferable to living and suffering on and on. What is the point? The end phase is no pleasure for anyone and slowly drags other lives into its black hole of emotional exhaustion. Not to mention personal energy, financial resources, and the inability to move on in life, or even maintain a normal life with friends and work and recreation— none of that is possible without death.

But death has another, more positive attribute. The dying person is not having the best experience, whatever stage of acceptance or denial he or she may be able to achieve. Death is not an athletic event where, if you can reach acceptance, you get a medal, and if you die angry or not at peace, you don't get a place on the podium. Regardless of the "blame the victim" roadmap for acceptance of death, fifty or more wonderful years ending in a few months of suffering is not a bad balance. However, my own enduring sorrow is not for my empty nest, loss of life partner, nor lowered standard of living. Whatever the standard, at least I'm living. Having life means having options and energy to seek new solutions—new ways to live. While I'm not happy now, interest in life and even happiness are possibilities I can pursue, and I think, at its root, life is about our passionate pursuits.

The person who has died is the person I feel sorry for, not myself. Nancy spent years fighting an ultimately futile, useless, demeaning, and painful fight against her intimate adversary—her own body. She kept up hope. She worked so hard to stay positive, do everything right, and work for recovery. She had achieved the life situation she'd worked for over decades. Now she had a lifetime of plans ahead of her, and she clung, at times desperately, ultimately tragically, to the hope she could live to enjoy that life and the work, volunteering, friends, and family that populated it. In addition, she suffered the slow realization of the inevitability she would fail in her life's most important struggle—a life versus death struggle going on inside of her. As Nancy's disease progressed, she adjusted to every new restriction and enjoyed what she could from every day left to her. She cleared up lingering relationship problems. She arranged family finances and found the emotional strength to enjoy her last visits from friends. She concerned herself with ensuring my financial and emotional well-being after her death.

So now, I'm to feel sorry for myself—after watching this person and what she went through as her body slowly consumed itself? That is impossible, and it's equally impossible to get over feeling pity and sorrow for her suffering—emotional more than physical.

What remedies can I think of to lessen my own pain for her? One is to remember the ratio—fifty-plus years of real life, with its experiences, fears, and phobias, triumphs, loves, losses, defeats, and trying again, versus eight months fighting the losing battle. And even within the eight months, we had some of our best times and grew closer together. We have never needed any more than time together to be happy—an exotic location or luxurious surround was a plus, but not all that interesting to either of us compared with the pleasure of time together any old place we could be away from the demands of our day-to-day working worlds.

But death is the other remedy. It cures all diseases. Whatever anguishes she suffered, they are completely erased now. She doesn't suffer those anguishes, and she doesn't live with debilitating scars of past suffering, except in the extent I might bear them vicariously.

As we live, we do accumulate complication, scars, suffering, and difficulties. We also accumulate calluses—webs of compensations and coping capabilities. wisdom and perspective for example— and the combination makes us more complete human beings, albeit increasingly complex ones. Death erases it all. It returns all that complexity to nature—to some extent transferring it to those who knew Nancy. But the rest is, in the more flexible sense of the word, entropy. A serious illness from which we recover can be life's way of rebooting. Death returns the entire hard disk to random ones and zeros. It is a necessary phase of the circle preceding creation of new order—planetary systems and people, which begin in randomness and grow into order.

We can think of that state of nothingness, of random ones and zeros, as a form of peace—a state free of strife, suffering, self-doubt, failure, loss, regret, pain, endless searching for answers that don't yet exist. Nancy is not suffering; only I am suffering. For her? There is no reason to suffer for her—she has given up her hold on suffering. She is well beyond its grasp, beyond the reach of even the concept. Death has granted her that blessing. And it has also granted it to me, even though I'm still alive. Death allows me, even while I'm among the living, the possibility to offload my burden of sorrow for her struggles and her losses. This is death's gift to me. Mine to accept if I want to, if I can truly understand death, and if I can learn to accept a gift from death, which I had always considered my ultimate enemy.

Because if I accept that gift, I have to admit that death is not completely my enemy. My war against death is not over, for it is in the nature of the living to deny and stave off death as our ultimate mission, or at least moderate it. Not a white flag, but a truce with death? I have to admit that my adversary has made an overture to me, and thus I have to question my ultimate, unconditional condemnation of death.

To learn, we must be prepared to let go of old ideas that prove incorrect, or, more often, to accept a higher level of complexity. A child may recognize right and wrong, but it takes mature, Solomonic wisdom to determine how right or how wrong a person may be in a complex human interaction where things are seldom black and white. A child knows death is bad, and it is the ultimate enemy. To grow, I have to realize that death is not one hundred percent bad. It can, at least in some instances, offer us possibilities. And possibilities are the essence of life—possibilities to live we could not have without death ever among us.

Death has made me an offer—a deal. If I will accept that death is not one hundred percent bad, if I will stop defaming death, despite its prominent role as a part of the natural world we believe was made for us by a perfect God, then I can have some larger share of life before my own arrival at my ultimate destination, which is death.

Which is all contained within the Kaddish. If we believe God created the universe, then surely death was part of the plan. We have the option to ignore it and live in only our present— like an animal to which the enlightenment of Eden was not granted. We can admit it, but fight it as enemy and be scared by the fragile reality of our existence. However, there is another possibility—to accept death as no more an enemy than a massive thunderstorm or a cold winter wind, which can be hurtful but is also a manifestation of the overpowering beauty all around us. I stand at the seaside in Rhode Island and at the same time see the ocean as beautiful and terrifying. I cannot swim through it to Europe because it would consume me and end my life. A giant wave could wash over me. The sea beckons us, but can easily overwhelm us.

I have spent fifty years ignoring death's reality, three years hating death as one hundred percent evil and as the enemy, fighting it emotionally, financially, technologically. And in defeat, as the one of our team of two that has come out the other side, I can see that all hatred, even hatred of death, harms the person who holds the hatred and has no effect on the object hated—has no effect on death. So while I can't say I have learned to love death, I have been led to understand death is a part of nature, a needed, even a comforting and welcome part, of nature's, or God's, gifts to us, the living. Death is my friend? For now, maybe my penpal.

Believing

In high school, when one of my fixations was Spanish, I read a classic slice of literature from Spain, Miguel de Unamuno's *San Manuel Bueno, Mártir*, about a Catholic priest whose secret was that he did not, could not, believe. His lack of ability to accept belief tortured him. It was a constant threat to, and in fact defined, his existence. Unamuno had himself similar problems with an inability to be that which he thought he should have been—initially as a Basque trying to be a Spanish literary figure. He was forever a misfit, despite all of his energy expended in being in some way more Spanish than most Spanish.

At the time I felt it was a literary device. Sure, there might be one idiosyncratic priest in a world of millions who had this problem, but is there anything interesting about one such person? There are all sorts of deviants in the world.

As an adult I realize how common Manuel's situation is. I have met many clergy personally who nowadays are free to admit that while they do not disbelieve, they doubt and really just don't know.

My scientific education also taught me that. And too few "scientists" get it. The appropriate mental state in the vast majority of situations is suspending judgment. Until there is truly a mountain of data, well worked through, it is impossible to know if cholesterol causes heart attacks, if global warming is real and caused by us, if people are fat because they eat too much and therefore people who are really fat are people who eat *way* too much. Since we do know the first is true, it's pretty tempting to extrapolate, but there is no "proof." Cigarettes seem to cause lung cancer, but how? Nobody knows.

The public hates this. They want to think there are answers and that we have good reasons to put rovers on Mars. Why spend a billion dollars if you don't even know why you're doing it? They want to think their religious leaders virtually commune with God at the pulpit—that they have answers. They want to think their authors, poets, and musicians see life more truly, and that their doctors know how to fix their bodies, their professors understand a subject completely, and that their countries really are doing it right.

But if you ask them about their own family—something they know better than anyone else, do they really know what they are doing with their kids, spouse, and parents? They know they are winging it. Some are better than others; some parents are highly experienced and believe they are good at it, yet the evidence suggests they may be confident, but may be performing no better than others.

So given all that, and all the people I've talked to about Nancy and the general situation of being dead, I have to accept the obvious conclusion. Nobody really knows, and it's doubtful we even have a clue. Some of us have confidence, and some—or all simultaneously—may be right. Or each may be creating her or his own reality just as valid as any other—which is the case for many religions. They are different, but they all work in the sense of providing us a way to live, with pluses and minuses of course, and a way to raise our sights higher, one hopes, or sometimes lower, unfortunately.

While I like my skepticism in other things, when it comes to faith I feel like that Spanish priest . I want to believe—or even disbelieve—anything to get a resolution. But I realize that's not the way I am. My strategy is to avoid the life of San Manuel and to get comfortable knowing that I won't be able to give myself a definite answer. I really hope Nancy sees the efforts I take on her behalf and on my own to do what I can with the life I got to have that she did not. But for some reason, I can't let myself one hundred percent believe it. A little voice keeps telling me, "Maybe you're wrong. Maybe it's something else entirely. Maybe it's nothing at all."

What does nothing mean? It means the way we think of a corn plant after the season, after it has given up its fruit, after it has shriveled up, and after the farm machines have pushed it back into the earth or collected it all and burned it. We don't believe each corn plant is still in its sun or watching over next year's crop from above. That's what I mean by nothing. I admit it as a possibility, though I don't believe it.

When Nancy died, even before she died, I realized there was a message aimed at me—that I had to realize that death is real. Both to be true to myself, and that, confronted with evidence, I had to set aside a belief in my own immortality. I had to respect her. It would trivialize her struggle if I dismissed death as merely a transition to a new place. Whatever would happen to her, it was not quite so simple as moving to a condo, maybe somewhere in Redondo Beach near the ocean and Trader Joe's, whose address and phone number I would never know. I set about thinking it's great to be a skeptic and believe nothing and sit on every fence. What do you believe? Is there any nugget at the center of all those specifics I can't believe that I personally believe?

What I see in others, one belief I have, is that most people have a belief. They may call it a "point of view." Whatever. So that's an easier question to answer. What is my "point of view"?

It's being an adult, being realistic and transitioning from a world of magical thinking that is a charming characteristic of younger people. Believing in infinite health, time, opportunity, that a great outcome is always possible if you apply yourself and get up and dust yourself off after life's setbacks is a useful and healthy model, and I don't discourage it. But my pivot point was to say, can I get beyond this magical thinking, confront the reality that it is not completely accurate? I was forced to see every hour of every day tending to Nancy, from her first serious treatment of chemotherapy in August 2007 to her death in April 2008.

I looked at photos of her—a healthy, always skeptical executive at a company picnic in July 2007 with no clue of what was just a few weeks in her future. That picnic—when she sat with Diet Coke under our big canopy and grumbled in her way of chiding me, about why in the world did we build a company in Virginia, the country's heat and humidity capital—would be one of her last days outdoors, except for transport between a car or ambulance and a hospital in a wheelchair or a stretcher. If this evolving story was not yelling in my ear to expand beyond my magical thinking, I was a scientist ignoring the data that seemed clearly to be incongruous with his model.

I told myself my belief had at least these two components:

One, there is a world beyond the magical thinking that had gotten me where I was today—the magical thinking that life will reward me if I keep trying, that opportunity is always there if

I keep looking for it and do my best to achieve the things that satisfy me, that I will always have the opportunity to fail and try again—which is essentially to say that ultimately there is justice and infinite opportunity. Life had to include the possibility of failure, and to still be worth living, to be both real and valid.

And two, that I can't accept a theory that works for people but not corn plants. I can't believe humans have a special spot in God's heart, and all of God's other creations—planets, universes, leaves, spiders, and corn plants, are discards—just props in a world built for humans. Even the most distant galaxies—those we don't know exist—are only there—these constructions which dwarf us, our world, our solar system, even our galaxy, do they only exist so that one of us earth-based humans might glimpse them for a few seconds some time thousands of years from now and put them in a catalog? That does seem to trivialize what appears to be a lot of the work of creation. No, I realized I believe life is not infinite and not necessarily just. And the universe is not here just for our benefit, the way a house and all its furniture we believe is all there just to shelter and comfort the people who dwell in it.

Even that obvious belief is untrue. The dogs and cats enjoy our houses. And if it's a famous person's house, Abraham Lincoln's cabin, or Renoir's Château des Brouillards, the house itself may become an inspiration to millions of people, or a home for millions of plants and animals. Even our tools have their own place in existence. They are not just our servants.

I do believe that one corn plant is simply a member of a community. It is a corn plant, but it is more than an individual. One corn plant, every corn plant, is one part of an infinite body of corn plants that extends all around the world and deep into history and far into our future. I see my own life the same way. I look at people on the road, on their Harley Davidsons, in a family car, driving a big ugly truck, or walking for exercise, and I think they are part of me, and I'm part of them. I experience a little of what they experience, if only by watching them. It is impossible to live all those lives, so the work is divided up and I have my little niche to pursue, but we are like this big army of humans, itself a division of a big army of living things, and that an element of a larger population of things that exist—which includes rocks, planets, etc., and all together we constitute some part of everything. Maybe everything is a part of an even bigger collection including things that no longer exist, that will exist in the future—even that will never exist. It seems a little far-fetched, this idea that a collection can contain things that will never exist, but it is not beyond possibility. So I don't rule it out. In fact, I think that's a great comfort. Even if Nancy does not exist at all, we are then still a part of this collection.

When I swim, I think of myself as a fish. I am, in some tiny fraction of my being, a fish. I think about how humans think they need arms to swim, and strong arms to swim fast. But fish are much faster—and hey, no arms. Fish live twenty-four/seven in water; their lives depend on swimming fast, and yet, no arms.

Sometimes I am a cat. No hands. No tools. A person in such a state we might call a paraplegic or disabled. But a cat is far from disabled. God, I hope I never have to live as a cat. A cat can't type, nor pick up a book. Yet what life a cat has—so many adventures, so much to do, such a refined sense of place and of touch and time.

Any tree or bush I pass I think—sure, it's a nice sunny day today, and it's easy being a tree. But that tree manages to survive day and night, summer and winter, ice storms, wind storms, dust and hail, salt trucks scattering ashes and potassium chlorate over its patch of ground. And yet, May comes, and the tree is green and luscious and welcoming. What a spirit that tree must have—to absorb these insults and yet to come back every year so happy, so proud, so free of guile. Humans aspire to that—we have that in common with a tree. Every bush is amazing in that way. I could never create such a thing. I couldn't make a single cell that could survive in perfect conditions in a lab. And yet here it is—just as ordinary as a rock, being what it is. Now I am that one. Though who knows? Maybe I'll have another life with a younger or healthier person who then has to die in the hands of a stranger, or of nobody. And who held Nancy's hand in her last minutes? Not me. I was in the shower. I'll never know if that was a poor use of time on my part—a subject I got straight "unsatisfactory" marks in all through elementary school, or Nancy's choice of how she wanted her life to end, or simply how the randomness of the universe played out one April pre-dawn, a few minutes after 5:00 a.m. I later had to fill out a form that included "time of death." I put a tilde before some digits, to indicate approximately. I didn't know.

Does it bother me that I may die without a hand holder? Not much—certainly not enough to endure raising a family only to increase the probability it won't happen. The fish will be swimming, the birds floating on their stream of air, there will be kids figuring out radio and electrons and ridiculous bike rides, the joys of overcoming a bad injury and coming back strong and smarter. All of my other existences—some will be gone; some new ones will be there. Even if we all would disappear in some gigantic global flu, the universe that built us would still be here and eventually rebuild something new.

If that tree were so fragile, there would be no trees. If life were so fragile as just our blue dot, there would be no life.

Our universe is never the same as it is right now, but neither is it heading for annihilation. If my tree were to die, I'd miss it. I'd mourn for it, and I mourn for all my immediate surroundings when I lose them—loss is no pleasure. I do what I can. I enjoy my relationships as best I can while I have them, my ability to go to some ridiculous staff picnic and complain about the humidity—while I can. There is no shelter from the storm of loss, except to realize that and to enjoy all the various transients we have the opportunity to experience. I enjoy my job as an infinitesimal part of the universe's army of existences and non-existences. What an opportunity—to share existence with the stars and galaxies, with the deer in the woods, and with the earth—and then maybe to not exist. These are great things. We can't understand any of them, and I am thankful to believe they will be there and that when that one thing that is me dies, it will make virtually no difference to this gigantic organism.

Well, I won't be happy about that. Nobody wants to die, but even less do I want to die not knowing how I feel about it. I would like to believe I personally will live forever and meet up with Nancy and all of my relatives. Frankly, I keep that option open. I plan to focus on that when I get close to the end. Losing Nancy has in that sense made my own end easier to accept. She did it. I can do it. And for all I know, my life now may be a forty-year business trip at the end of which I'll be back together with her, back to comfortably ignoring each other— her docked in front of her big TV with a Diet Coke, me writing at my computer nearby, each of us in our own, barely touching, universes. We'll ride again in the blue Miata, and she'll first ask me why I love that bucket of bolts and then ask me if I can steer it to a heading better for drenching her face in the spring sun, as if I can change the layout of the street and the earth's orbit about our sun.

And maybe it won't be that way. But all of the things of which I am a part, I know will still be there—other existences. Ayn Rand did not believe that. She believed when she closed her eyes, the universe disappeared. Maybe she was right, though she has closed her eyes, and I believe I still exist. My belief that the universe goes on is not provable, but it is my belief. And it is my belief that I will never know what is true so long as I am alive, and that I'm free to believe what I want to and keep all those options open. I can hope for one or another. I hope I rejoin Nancy and my friends and family in death, and continue to have new experiences, but I accept that maybe I won't.

For me, it's more comforting to not know, to have existence in common with all of us, and to be a part of the stream, than to not fully believe even something I would so much like to believe.

How It Is

You're enjoying a weekend on a rented sailing sloop, not far from the Indonesian shore when a sudden storm capsizes the little boat. You are sure to die out there, but you spot a small island and swim to its beach. The weather is warm, lots of banana trees: fruit for eating, leaves for clothing and, if not shelter, at least cover so you can sleep on the beach. For the next few days, you work furiously to find and store sufficient food, build a semi-permanent shack to get out of the sun, rain, and cool evening breeze, and eventually get a fire going.

You make a lot of mistakes—get cut, get infected, worry, but get over it. The fire goes out overnight in a rain shower, and the next day it's too wet to start a new one, so you're cold for most of the day. But eventually you dry out and start again. You make a crude net out of banana leaves and catch a fish in it—cook it over the fire on a stick.

You consider yourself lucky. You survived. And immediately reconsider yourself unlucky. Life is going to be subsistence, alone on this island.

Sometimes, when the fire is healthy, you have enough bananas and leaves, the shed is reinforced from the last storm, and you have a moment before heading to the shore with your fish net. You scan the sky for passing aircraft. You examine the horizon for ships that might be visible above the chop.

Then it's back to fishing...

Lulu Is Sick

The vet and I were trying to pin my cat down on the simulated granite examining table. Dehydrated, vital functions all indicating she might not make it, under the bright lights and in the gloved hands of the vet, Lulu, who had been virtually limp since I awoke to check her at 3:00 a.m., momentarily reenergized herself, instinctively trying to get away. She squirmed, and as I tried to hold her, I realized her fur was damp. It was raining hard that morning, the way I experienced it for the first time during my freshman year in college in Providence. An intensity I've theorized for thirty-five years signaled our proximity to the Atlantic Ocean. The core of my personal rain theory is that in Rhode Island when it rains in torrents, the air smells of seaweed. Maybe it's the Northeast wind bringing in the water and the salty air that hugs the cold ocean's surface. This morning it had soaked me, and even penetrated Lulu's pet carrier, but she was, until now, too weak to seem to care.

It's a fine line—holding her with enough strength to let her know there's no point in squirming, not so much that it might hurt. She got the message of my damp fingers, hands and arms, and stopped struggling, standing with her signature broad stance on the table, allowing the vet to check her from end to end, including her teeth and gums, even her eyelids. She whimpered and looked up at me. Was I just projecting into her viridian eyes the question: What is happening to me?

It is not the first time I've looked into the other's eyes and saw the question that doesn't want to know the answer. It is unforgettable. And in that moment, my emotions, my pity for every one of those pairs of asking eyes, and the lost companion who can't, who doesn't, have an answer, chilled me in a way even the heaviest Rhode Island rain never could.

My mind searched its catalog of other animals I have seen suffering. A raccoon, dragging her broken leg across the bike path on a late autumn afternoon, haunted me that evening after my ride home as I sat in front of my computer in my bright and heated suburban house. Where would she find a warm dry bed, a sling to brace her fracture, and food? Who would comfort her? Would she have a bible to read about Job, so that she could recognize the nobility of her suffering? Could she drink some warm tea and swallow two aspirin? More likely, a fox would find her an easy dinner, or she would die of her wounds and their complications.

One winter day during the time Nancy's illness was closing in on her, I went out on my bicycle for one of those caregiver breaks we fortunate ones tell ourselves we deserve. Climbing a hill in just below freezing air under a featureless sky, I saw a grey squirrel by the side of the road, oblivious to cars going by and to me. Unusual for a squirrel, usually hyper aware and hair trigger. As I came by, climbing slowly up a ten percent grade at maybe seven miles per hour, I saw he was nudging another squirrel with his nose. The other squirrel had just recently been hit by a car—the blood was bright red and freshly flowing on the ground. The healthy squirrel kept nudging the dead squirrel's head and body, trying to get him to wake up, move, or respond.

Any observer would recognize what was happening. The live squirrel was beginning the experience of loss. This little creature didn't yet understand or didn't want to his mate was not going to wake up. Eventually his own survival imperatives would force him to move on, and he would at some level come to accept that his relationship with the other squirrel, and his own life as he had come to know it, were over.

I could do nothing for the raccoon. Nor for the squirrel. I can no more help them live their lives or do anything for the dead or the dying than I could swim with the fish in the ocean. At most, the fish and I are tangent for an instant during my hour swims paralleling the beach. But I am a prisoner of the surface, while they quickly fin their way deep into the cold and dim salt water farther from shore. I resolved to be more present in the world I do inhabit, to be more empathetic with people, and to care more for them and for myself.

Now in this moment, Lulu and I are the two orthogonal lives, tangent for the instant of her plaintive glance into my eyes. I remembered my resolution to help if I could. I failed to change any of the tragic outcomes I've witnessed—not the raccoon, not the squirrel, not Nancy. I am hopeless at defending vegetarianism to a world convinced that meat is imperative, despite my life and so many others who avoid killing animals as evidence to the contrary. I've never saved a life, human or other, and I don't know how I could. I'm not going to let Lulu get away from me, but I've learned, despite what the plaque at the base of the monument on the Green at Brown University states. Love is *not* strong as death. I bargain that whatever the outcome of the struggle is, Lulu will know I am with her. I stare back at her. We are going to get through this, I transmit to her, fully aware the whole dialog I'm engaged in is crazy.

Lulu's energy subsides. With a quieter whimper this time, her body settles onto the hard surface, accepting whatever will be.

The vet takes advantage of the momentary lull to leave the room, fetching medications and a syringe. I can relax my grip. How do we talk to animals? How do we reach anyone through the leaden veil of suffering? Even among humans, there are no words. The only real communication is your presence near them, your vigilance, the sense of your caring, sharing space and breath. Like Morse code, companionship can penetrate where the noise of language cannot. Human language is not communication, I realize in the middle of all this. It is negotiation, carrying out the business of day-to-day life. While the lips speak, they cannot kiss. Wordless presence is basic, essential, the only true communication between souls.

I hold my hands gently around Lu's damp body. Freed of my tight grip, she slowly, deliberately, extends her left front paw, stretching it forward, finally resting it on my wrist. A single, still life, not knowing what will be. We wait.

Lulu Results

I promise not to bug you all anymore about Lulu, but thought I would at least send the results.

In three days we went from a vet diagnosis of "no big deal," to my thinking, early on Sunday morning, that maybe this actually was a big deal. I had a long trip in the rain and dark to get her to the ER. With help from my dad and his new portable GPS, I was able to find a small place on a big road in bad visibility. The new diagnosis was she is a "very sick kitty" (that's the technical jargon). It was unlikely Lulu would make it without extreme and uncertain measures, possibly resulting in a permanent disability (maybe dialysis for a cat?) Later in the day the diagnosis changed again. Lulu had an operable condition. From there, we decided to go for it. That was Monday. Tuesday I picked her up from surgery, twenty-four hours post-op.

So my Zen cat is home and enjoying life again. She had two big stones in her bladder, but that's a routine surgery (routine does not equal cheap nor comfortable), and she looks like any human post-op. She has fur shaved off at the site of surgery (lower abdomen), and about eight large surgical steel staples. She also has fur shaved off where they had ECG monitors, and one leg where they had an IV inserted (yes, they do IV drugs for cats). She gets antibiotics twice per day for a week prophylactically, and I have pain meds if she gets uncomfortable, which so far she isn't. I also have one of those circus clown cones in case she starts pulling at the staples. If she does, she's tougher than I am.

The prognosis is she'll be one hundred percent fine. She has a new diet with a mix of dry and canned (or nowadays the trend is to foil wrap) wet food, and a new bubbler thing that makes water a little more interesting. Cats like to drink moving water, and this thing sort of makes the water burble. It's a little like an aquarium pump, only no air—it just pumps the water around. It's what I would call a Zen fountain.

It's a little ironic how much I learned from caring for Nancy that, subconsciously, I transferred to Lulu. I think we all do that with our pets—project our own ways of being or ways we'd like to be. Death is a big thing. If you let it win, you have to live with that forever, which, as the song says, is a long time. Win or lose, you do both yourself and the patient a mitzvah by engaging in the fight. This time the good guys won.

Another lesson I had learned was, when somebody comes home from the hospital, they need bling (or in the case of males, gadgets). Lulu has a new heart-shaped bronze charm to replace the old one that had my old cell phone number and other outdated details on it. She also got the water gadget, but like most females, is disinterested. In addition, she has good food. All patients like upgraded menu options.

Lulu is resting comfortably, waking up to eat, slurp a little water, get brushed, purr, and curl up again. I doubt she had slept from Saturday to Tuesday.

Anyway, I think we're beyond crisis point, and I appreciate all your support. I realize Lulu is just a cat, but as humans, we have a responsibility to try to do right by the animals we bring into our worlds, take responsibility to care for, and who, for their part, bring an added dimension to our lives. I maintain a hope that people who own pets might eventually change their feelings about other animals, despite that historical trends don't appear to justify my optimism. I'm glad we were able to help out Lulu. She has certainly earned at least this much.

—Rick

Asking Why

One theory of the universe is there is not one, but an almost infinite number of universes. Here are two more theories:

You lead a major proposal effort to win that next big contract. You spend more money than your company can afford. Many people think you're on an irresponsible path to destroying the entire enterprise, but you see a once-in-a-lifetime opportunity to break out. One day, an envelope arrives and you open it.

In one universe, you've grabbed the big brass ring. You're a hero, toasted at the win party. The Board loves you, the employees love you, and the shareholders love you. You are a visionary.

In another, you're a bumpkin. You're never given that responsibility again. You humbly return to your previous status of company nebbish. They don't fire you. That would be too generous. Rather, you keep your head low in your cubicle and hope, if not for mercy, for anonymity.

Every day an uncountable number of outcomes occur—car accidents, encounters with old friends, wrong numbers dialed, or glass stepped on. You might oversleep and show up late for an interview, but it provides an opportunity to show you can recover. Your immune system fights off a bug, or not, resulting in a week in bed or missing a week of work. In some of the cases where you succumb, it gets out of hand and you die, or you just infect everyone else in the house and they all miss a week of school or work. Each one of these events branches out into a new set of alternative universes. Imagine how many universes would be created per second, with billions of people and uncountable other creatures each doing things moment by moment. But infinity is big enough to contain any number of universes, which makes this bizarre theory not provably wrong.

The web of alternative universes is not navigable. Even our single universe is not knowable. It's impossible to know what paths of the universe we are tracking and where they will lead us, let alone all those billions of alternative universes and their propagation paths

When your most beloved dies, your eyes are opened. You are forced to realize the impermanence of everything. Of course, you always knew that in a logical sense. If someone asked you where will you be in one hundred years, you'd know the answer—dead and gone. But until a big loss occurs, that's a complete abstraction you construct walls around, like a little nugget of kryptonite, and you live comfortably knowing that box is there, but isn't affecting you at the moment. Your loss breaches the box. Now it is not just abstract, but real. At times a rapid dissolution into your eventual fate might seem even preferable to life without that person.

Your gaze penetrates deeply into depths you didn't want to see. You liked living in the warm shallows. You were comfortable swimming the sunlit reefs of daily life with its bike rides, meals with friends, ocean swims, rock music, and comforts of home, family, and friends. You don't want to see the dark, unlit depths where the big predators are swimming and hunting those cold and quiet waters. You have your first experience in a new and frightening world, a reality more real than your present, temporal state. The shallows now seem an illusion of a previous life. You spend time lost among the alternative universes you never before thought about—the lands of what if.

What if you had caught the disease sooner? What if you had been more aggressive and tried that other therapy instead of this one? Or made the trip to the famous medical center? What if you had made one more phone call or chosen a route off the main road? What if the ambulance arrived sooner? What if you'd had that one more test, chosen a different hobby, kept your child in home-schooling, had that operation when you were still young or well enough to endure it, or had eaten more broccoli? What about the $600 you didn't spend for ABS and traction control, or that job you didn't take in the South where they don't have snow, or in the East where the earthquake probability is lower? Was that trip necessary at all? Can't politicians work a little harder before calling up their armies? Had the disease struck ten years later, a cure would have been available, cheap, and effective.

And if death was inevitable, a proposition impossible to accept, what if you had been a better parent or spouse or friend; what if you hadn't economized on that last vacation; what if you didn't have that last fight over nothing? What if you had spent less time at work or in front of the laptop and spent more time in dinner conversation? What about all those movies you didn't see together? Why not? Or the gift you hadn't yet given, the words not yet spoken, the financial success that had always eluded you, your child's graduation? Couldn't we have lived together for just one more milestone?

We can never know what is down all those roads. We can't even see a day ahead on the road we're on. Had you not had those fights, it wouldn't have been your life and their life and your relationship. It would have been a Disney version. You could have flown all over the planet for a cure, only to exhaust your energy and bank balance and spoil your last months together in a fruitless, disappointing, quixotic mission. Find it sooner and suffer even more months of anxiety? Any number of disasters could have happened in that universe when you lived in the earthquake-free Midwest—a tornado, a tainted tomato, a drunk driver.

I don't believe that outcomes are completely beyond human control. What we do matters. Otherwise, why pursue engineering, medicine, or science if the human condition has already been written in a book we can only read? But neither do we control many big things. There's a Yiddish expression for our predicament of wishing we had navigated into a universe where we would have avoided our loss and our beloved's suffering: *Mann traoch, Gott lauch.* Man plans, God laughs.

But how could God allow the suffering of an innocent person—maybe a child? Now you find yourself reading thick philosophical tomes and thin pop-psyche pabulum—the infinite domain of the irrational where there is no map, no simple formula that spits out the answer. There are thousands of proposals, many created by humanity's greatest intellects, but none of them any more than a convenient lens to imperfectly look at the unseeable, unknowable future. Like soaking in salt water to extract toxins, there's no harm in immersing your mind in all that thought and speculation until your skin is wrinkled and you just can't wait to get out of the tub.

The wind is much stronger than I am. There are days it gusts so strong, it's impossible to make progress on a bicycle or even stay upright. There is weather you and your aircraft are not going to penetrate in one piece. God is greater than I am, greater than my aircraft, my muscles, and machines. He is greater than my planning and my theories of the nature of all things. The only choices are exhaustion, fighting, or awaiting a better day.

Our only win strategy is to keep on keeping on. Eventually, a cold front will push through, and I'll coast in a massive tailwind. The skies will clear and freezing rain will be hard to imagine ever existed. And in those beneficent intervals, we'll rebuild our travels, our itineraries, our plans, our temples, our houses, our relationships, our families, and our lives.

Entropy, the process of everything unwinding, is inexorable, but it is not the whole story. The human will can rebuild. Some of those great thinkers of the ancient world concluded that is our shared human mission—"Tikkun ha-Olam," which means to rebuild the world that is constantly subject to erosion by chaos. And in that rebuilding, we experience God. We don't understand why wind, rain, and entropy fight us, but they are all part of the universe that was made for us to dwell in. One day we touch the wall ten milliseconds sooner and grab the bronze, and another day we crouch in our cubicle, the thin envelope cast aside but nonetheless the biggest object in the office. Our only choice is to keep building. The effort may or may not be futile. We can never know if what we do can make a difference—that is written only in the unfolding of the many virtual universes yet to be selected. It is only faith, the floating plank we cling to, that doing is preferable to not doing. However, while we soak in salty waters, doing distracts us from the sting.

Stop Writing

I keep saying I have to stop writing this book. Then I keep writing it, despite that I have way too many other things to do. How many times one says one's going to quit anything vs. actually quits? (Ten percent of people who try to quit smoking succeed for a year. Three percent of all smokers quit per year—at least for a year.)

Nancy used to chide me, "Do you do any work for a living?" But her better observation was that, like my eating, I do a lot of work. I just don't get paid for most of it. In eating—I do a lot of that, but mostly foods that don't have much in them. Watermelon, for instance.

But I digress.

This is really it. Somehow I thought this might be a good wrap-up for the whole opus. I figure if I write the last essay, I can license myself to lay off and get back to my real job—as soon as I figure out what that is, Or maybe the next book. I guess the reality is, it will take a month or two to organize all this.

—Rick

The 5 O'Clock Sun

Magical thinking is not limited to great spiritual matters. My family believes in the five o'clock sun, a necessity to get through long spells of grey skies shading the darker grey slushy streets of Cleveland, our landscape from November to April. We believe that the sun will not completely abandon us. We deserve a few minutes at that perfect time when Sol slides sideways toward the horizon and shines directly into the kitchen window, gold and sparkling on the papered walls and wood cabinets. Clouds cannot be everywhere. The sun can peak through the voids in its fabric. We will enjoy our moment in the sun. Setting in the West, where our weather convects from, the five o'clock sun demonstrates clear skies are on the way. During summer, storms may close the pool all day. We don't mind because we plan to swim at five o'clock, when the sun will make the ripples sparkle and dry the concrete deck. The turbulent atmosphere of daytime draws water from Lake Erie and creates the clouds of the day. Evening brings calm. The clouds dissipate, and for a few minutes we could be in Sacramento.

Who knows the five o'clock sun? Only we, who are always outdoors, watching for it, ready to greet it, to swim, bike, walk the dog, or grill hamburgers outside in its reassuring illumination. Or those of us who, in Virginia, bike a hundred and ten miles out to the Blue Ridge and back as a way to reduce life to weather watching and pedaling, to metering out water, food, and exertion in just the right measures, and to modulating clothing to stay comfortable as the wind, the terrain, the air temperature, and the level of effort follow their cycles.

Virginia, with ocean rather than mountain to its east, doesn't often have the gift of five o'clock sun. It's sunny here all day, sometimes many days in a row, but that's not conceivable in Northeast Ohio along the Lake Erie. But today in Virginia it rained all day—a Cleveland rain, not heavy like the Nor'easters in New England, not cold like the storms that descend on California from the Gulf of Alaska. Not impulsive like the waves of rain that soak the Mediterranean countries, punctuated by longer periods of warm sun, or like the cycling of rain/sun/rain/sun of England. Today, steady, fine drops slowly soaked everything, and a featureless grey sky completed the watery calm. The closest a human might experience to the life of a fish, the water is everywhere, soft and supportive, defining your ecology.

At five o'clock I was back in civilization on the last few miles when the objective is to avoid cars, buses, pedestrians, potholes. Pilots know the flight isn't over until the airplane is chocked on the ramp and the passengers are inside the terminal. Just then, the sun blinked at me, at my suburbia, from beneath the deck of grey, lighting up the bottoms of the clouds, the raindrops still falling from them, streaming from windshields, down my jersey. The street gleamed, so proud of its black asphalt and safety orange stripes. I rode a Japanese lacquered street that lacked only an inlaid crane of jade.

I looked away from the sun to the east, and there was a perfect rainbow, like a child's picture-book rainbow, printed on raindrop paper. As the sun separated farther from the clouds, a second Roy G. Biv arc appeared to accompany the first. They hung there, two companions visiting us in the sky, perfect from one anchor point just over the next hill to the other behind the K-Mart shopping center. Maybe because the sun was so close to the horizon, the four bases of the two arcs were thick, most heavily saturated with their colors, and vibrating. I had to remind myself to watch the street and the traffic and only steal glances at the lights and the colors. I watched the drivers in the oncoming cars. They could not see the rainbow because their windshields and car seats were pointing the wrong direction. And my fellow southeast-bound travelers? They seemed equally oblivious to the show. Was I imagining? I took my Oakleys off my eyes with my left hand. The rainbow sparkled and pulsed as the rain changed its moods to bigger and smaller drops, heavier and lighter, and the wind blew it around. The others on the road *must* be seeing it. Maybe they too are busy focusing more on crash avoidance than entertainment. If so, that might be a good thing.

There is nothing at the end of the rainbow, and the climax of a five o'clock sun is the darkness of a winter evening. Should I mind a rainy day, when every leaf sparkles to me as I ride by, slick and shiny, and when the light is soft as a polished cotton blanket and my face is moisturized with infinitesimal droplets? Enormous energy is required to separate water into smaller and smaller droplets. All that work—to what great purpose, if not to create a special underwater world for those of us who live on the land, not beside it under the water's solid surface? The poems and songs are wrong. Rain is wonderful; it is a release from the solid phase we are otherwise banished to. It changes everything and gives it a new life. Why should anything be at the end of a rainbow? Has the rainbow failed us because we laid an expectation of gold and riches upon it that it knows nothing about? It soars over woods, fields, and K-Mart without discrimination. It soars high into the five o'clock sky, huge, sparkling billboard advertising: five o'clock sun!!! Free! Today only!

Is anybody buying it? In this new age we keep our hands and our wallets in our pockets. Life is hard. Hang on to your pennies. Not me. I'm buying the five o'clock sun, the twenty-three hours of clouds that make it possible, and while I'm at it, the whole billboard, complete with zero return on investment. I spent my whole Saturday to buy it. I have no buyer's remorse.

Now northbound for the last mile on Reston Parkway, the air is drying, the rainbow is evaporating with the droplets. Only its golden base, now anchored somewhere around Route 7, remains—a giant, golden brick, always about to impact earth, zero mass at the speed of light. It releases me, and I coast down my cul-du-sac to welcome the darkness, like the day's greyness—soft, isotropic, and featureless.

Return of the Spies

Courtesy David Ascalon of Ascalon Studios

Low Tide

It's low tide. The deer family that lives near the RI house , with whom Nancy bonded and used to coo to when they'd come by to lunch on our bushes, is crossing the salt pond to reach the islands. They splash through the waves, which are only about knee-high for them, twice per day.

Nancy always wanted me to tell her if I spotted them, even if she was asleep. They are huge deer. The buck is much bigger-looking than my Miata. His eyes are like the objective lens of binoculars, and his ears are big and luxuriant. When the deer stare, they hold their ears at attention. Their senses have an unmistakable intensity, all about survival in the North. That's when I miss her. When something she enjoyed so much happens, I want to say, "Hey—there they are—your deer family." They came by the other day and stared up at me, four grey statues, while I put laundry out to dry on the deck. Were they looking for Nancy? I like to think so.

Afterword

Athletes use their bodies as board pieces in a game. We place them on top of gossamer frames with two wheels held together by a sparse spider web of spokes, and propel them down mountainsides at fifty miles an hour, mix in traffic with cars twenty, thirty times their mass. Swimming, running, tennis, basketball—we extend the body's joints, twist them, strain our muscles for an extra inch. It's no wonder most of society is sedentary. Maybe they have a certain rationality we lack. And it's also no wonder we get hurt. I've spent maybe two years of my life in casts, on crutches, wearing slings and braces, meeting doctors to talk about heavy-duty readings of my MRI images. I even spent a few months in a wheelchair.

Some of the lessons of sport, winning and losing, more often just training, injury, disability and recovery, have helped me through this year. If nothing else, a bike ride can be the best therapy on a down day. For people who have never had the experience, recovery from a disability can be an exhilarating experience. You look back on six difficult months. It was hard enough just to get through a working day without normal abilities, lugging crutches and casts around with you all day and finding some way to get to work and back—and then facing what the physical therapists call the "activities of daily living." Every shower, if you are lucky enough to be able to shower, every article of clothing to be taken off or put on, every dish to be washed, every pile of junk mail that needs to find a wastebasket or recycling bin, has been a challenge. Before walking from study to kitchen, you take stock of what other errands could be accomplished so as to not have to do it twice. Add to that the doctor visits, exercise regimen, drugs, gadgets to buy and learn to help do the otherwise un-do-able. It's a challenge beyond a mere Iron Man. And there is no medal, no all-you-can-eat watermelon, and no kiss at the finish line.

Now here you are out on the bike, enjoying the sunshine, the wind, and each little up and down hill. It's as if it were all a long and complex novel you read in French for Lit class, looking up every third word in your LaRousse. Today you graduated, and your body gave you an A. The lesson of life, over and over since your first stubbed toe when learning to walk the stairs, is recovery and growth.

Death has a different message, and that message, a year into my own process, is symmetry. We are born with nothing, and the tragedy of death to the dying person and to the living is loss. The dying person sees death as the process of eventually giving up every object, every relationship, every comfort and pleasure. Even the memory of those things, even the ability to care about that memory is stripped. You are undergoing a process that brings you back to the state of possession you had before birth. All those things you accrued are being returned. Let's not pretend that Buddhism or Judaism or books on how life transcends death change the fact that we don't willingly give all that up. Life transcending death may be statistically true because life has outlived the individual longevity by billions of years, but to the individual this theory can be interesting but is not particularly comforting. We are wired to the pursuit of life and don't find coming to grips with its end naturally within our nature. Maybe it can be learned, but at best, you are speaking French, a language you may have learned well or not so well, but it not your mother tongue. Our mother tongue is living, not dying.

A lifetime of setbacks and recovery has to be unlearned in order to accept that death is also a part of living—as common as entering kindergarten or as getting your driver's license. There are more funerals than weddings. Yet when we think of milestones of life, we don't think of hospice and death. If we do, they are way down the list behind relatively unusual events, like a sweet sixteen party, a bat mitzvah at age seventy-five, or a pilgrimage to Mecca.

What about those of us lucky enough to survive and to have the opportunity to face the challenge of going on in life after loss? Again, I think life's lessons, of injury and recovery, may be a form of selective learning, if not magical thinking, and is certainly an idealization of what life really has to say to us. But if we truly believe that words of the Kaddish, that God is good and perfect and has created the ideal universe for us, despite our convictions to the contrary when faced with loss, then we should have the courage to see life as it really is, without needing to filter it through the lens of expectation, idealism, even narcissism. We must ourselves be like the dying person, completely exposed down to the skin and below, to what is the entirety of human experience.

In fact, not all injured athletes do recover. However, those I've met, even with permanent disabilities, and always from freak events that would have not even occurred except for some bizarre split second mistiming of events, seem to eventually find a new deal with life, a way to live and even to love life. They are living the fact that people do recover, and to the extent they don't, they are capable of bridging the rest of the gap with their amazing adaptability. Even the idealist in us can see the wisdom of the Kaddish, despite tragedy, God, nature, and evolution, or however you model that which brought us to this state. Has not that tragedy, God, nature, and evolution, whatever, given us a life in Eden, given us a gift to go on and continue our lifelong quest for happiness, accomplishment of personal goals, and satisfaction, in part *because* of our setbacks?

They say the caregiver dies with the dying. This is true and even desirable. Wouldn't each of us have gladly taken that person's place so that they could live on in the state of health we still enjoy a year later? I'm living in Rome now, overworked, waking up before 3:00 a.m. to write before long, gritty days teaching, consulting, riding the metro and the bus, and walking the cobblestone streets on crutches while recovering from a silly bike crash—a slip on ice on a sunny spring day with temperatures in the fifties. Nancy has none of that. She lives only in my dreams, and the thoughts of her mother and sisters and brother, and maybe some friends who remember her and who are part of our small community, who help each other to learn to accept and go on and find new happiness, and to not feel guilty that we have the good fortune to be able to take up life's struggles.

The death of the caretaker is also true on another level. For me, a lifetime addict to training, mental and physical, to the setbacks that go with any attempt to do new things—race faster, speak Italian, achieve some other college degree, and to sticking with it and eventually overcoming those setbacks, symmetry—that every thing, every ability, we accumulate in life we ultimately must give up,—is a lesson I was long overdue for.

Others told me I'll never get over losing Nancy. I agreed rationally. I have no desire to forget or to somehow put in a neat box of logic, that Nancy had to die, and die as she did. But my nature told me the time after her death would be another difficult period, and I would transcend it.

Tonight is the last of my weekly anniversaries of Nancy and of my last night sharing her room, when I cared for her, fed her shaved ice, watched inane videos on her Mac, cleaned her skin and made her pillows just so, brushed her sparse head of sandy brown blonde hair, reported the inane news of the day and the greetings of friends, the cards that had arrived, the flowers, before yet another major milestone: today, in the month it ended, one year after the night it ended, the morning I found her as I had never seen a person in my fifty-three years of living—motionless and without life, but otherwise exactly as I'd left her an hour before. It has been a year of these milestones— the first week, the first month, three months. The first of all the annual cycle of holidays, the first trip to the Rhode Island house, to New York, to Europe, to our shared work place at the company I since sold but have returned to, everything identical except for the absence of her and of me. The absence of us.

What is it I can tell you I can share with Nancy, given the gulf between us—the gulf between existence and non-existence? What hubris to think a human can stand in both those worlds. We share the permanence of death, the reality of symmetry. People without the experience see analogies with injuries, with loss of a house, a job, a friend, or a lover. Eventually they earn back some of those possessions lost in their personal economic crisis, or adapt to the simplicities of living with less. They meet new friends and lovers. The past becomes a stage set for a present perceived, if not better, at least satisfactory. But if you see life and death as they really are, or since none of us can do that, at least with clear eyes, you do not return to the garden of asymmetry. You have seen the rest of the story in one year, compared with decades living an illusion, a selective vision of growth, recovery, and improvement. You don't speak the new language fluently. You are an immigrant to a strange new land,

and you have picked up some vocabulary. You can conjugate a few verbs, but it's not effortless, natural, rich, and fast, this new language.

But it is—can I say *interesting*? You have dreams—strange dreams, insightful dreams, dreams you thought yourself incapable of imagining. You think about spiritualism in a new way. You are conscious that we humans believe we know much more than we possibly can know in order to feel control over that which we can not even control—even see what is around the corner five minutes ahead of us. At best, we control very minor things, but the biggest events are beyond our control or even our understanding. It is concrete. Loss is a facet of life shared by billions of people. You understand others' loss just a little bit. Sometimes you can help them in ways you couldn't before, until that uncomfortable new dimension was etched on your consciousness.

A year on, what is the message I am receiving from living beyond death? Like the athlete with the injury from which she won't recover, eventually the irrationality of the complex experience we call loss, while a puzzle we cannot resolve, becomes less important than the stretch required of my brain to accommodate a less-than-perfect return to where I was before. I hear stories of deaf people whose identity includes their deafness so completely that they refuse medical treatments that might restore their hearing. Many, not all, of the community of loss, me included, feel the same way. Do I want to remarry, re-occupy a few houses and apartments and offices scattered around the world, commuting among them and rendez-vousing wherever on weekends? Or shared dinners at home in front of the TV and PC, watching Groundhog Day?

No. If some of that happens, it happens, but laying hardwood over a Pirelli floor of the peaks and valleys of loss, wallpapering over loss, is not my plan. Loss is a hard language to learn, and while I'm struggling to speak other languages, I don't want to lose the little bit of facility I have earned with it.

Not everyone learns French or Italian or Japanese, travels to interesting places with high standards of living, interesting technologies, and great food. Sometimes we learn the languages of countries where one lives on dirt, eats minimal sustenance, and spends the day on routine, almost trivial tasks that would be handled by simple machines or by others back at home. We don't love those places less. In a way, we love them more, because the ability to be able to enjoy them is so hard-won and so rewarding. We can cross that wide gap and reach out to others who live there, who welcome companionship much more than an Italian surrounded by his cars, cellular phones, wideband internet, overcrowded streets and trattorias, and sixty-one FM stations crammed into 20 MHz.

It is a year since the loss came to completion, two years since the process started with an unsuccessful surgery to remove Nancy's disease, and an intervention that had worked so well for so many years. Seven hundred and thirty-one days. A baby grows from an egg in nine months, about the same time it takes to grow a new bone after a bike crash. A baby needs two years of life to learn its first language. As adults, we lose that facility because our first language is already in the prime spot in the brain, reserved for the mother tongue.

But in two years of daily lessons, I can at least navigate the streets and learn to survive in the land of loss and to speak with the others who live here. After all, we are all immigrants in a strange land, and none of us is fluent. Have I recovered? Have I wanted to "recover"? That word doesn't exist here. We are free of it, free of the illusion of permanence, free of the security of our things, our friends, free of Linus's blanket. Sure we long for it, as any immigrant longs for a visit to the home country to speak that now apparently ancient language the natives still chatter on in, leading their peculiar lifestyles as if they were the way God built the universe and as natural as air. We hover an inch above credulity.

Through bad luck, or my own clumsiness, I can't touch the ground, even, through a filament, as a cyclist floats above the ground, but senses its presence transmitted through a web of filaments, bicycle spokes. Nancy built for me a filament from earth to infinity. Can I stretch the gap to symmetry, to where she is? Almost. In my dreams. I speak Italian like a native. However, I know I'm not ready to give up my Americanism, my running shoes, khaki trousers, or v-neck sweater, or fluency in the language and culture of twenty-first century America.

Now I do not question death, life. I have one question only—can I stretch a filament across just that one inch that synapse from here to what was once the logic of my life?

.